THE

Beauty

(of)

BUSINESS

A COMPLETE GUIDE FOR WOMEN IN DIRECT SELLING

Cyndi Kaplan

Godiva Publishing Pty. Ltd.
Sydney, Australia.

International Edition

Cyndi Kaplan 1992

First published in 1992
Second Edition 1993
Godiva Publishing Co Pty Ltd
3/6 Fullerton Street
Woollahra 2025 NSW Australia
Phone: (02) 326 2507
Fax: (02) 327 2501

Kaplan, Cyndi, 1952
The Beauty of Business: A Complete Guide for Women in Direct Selling

National Library of Australia Cataloguing-in-Publication entry:
ISBN O 646 10869 7

1. Women in business.
2. Women in direct selling.
3. Success in business.
4. How to set up a direct selling career.
5. A review of direct selling companies in Australia.

Photograph of Cyndi by Michael Freiman
Typeset by Character & Caps Sydney and The Albion Place Group Sydney
Cartoons by Max Foley
Cover design by Gail Reingold
Printed and bound by The Book Printer
Distributed by National Book Distributors
190 Roger Street
Brookvale 2100 NSW Australia
Phone: (02) 905 7855
Fax: (02) 905 7923

DEDICATION

Dedicated to my wonderful
children Jason and Nikki
whose lives continue to enrich
and inspire me.

To my friend, soulmate
and love Michael,
thank you for being
the wind beneath my wings.

ACKNOWLEDGEMENTS

Heartfelt thanks to the executive director of the Direct Selling Association of Australia, John Fulton for his ongoing support, help and positive input; to all the Australian direct selling companies who gave so willingly of their time to make this book possible; to the wonderful women I interviewed, thank you for sharing. Thank you also to Graeme Spry, John Nevin and Helen Bruveris for sharing their expertise. To the many people who helped me bring this book from an idea to the finished product: Ngiarie for her typing, Di Alperstein and Della Fuchs for their time and effort in editing, Anne O'Callaghan for her great service in the printing process, a special thanks to Sue Bredow for her editorial input in turning my dream to reality and to Karen Brady for her initial inspiration.

Sydney, August 1992

CONTENTS

FOREWORD

As the Direct Selling Association of Australia Inc. celebrates its 25th Anniversary we read in this book why the direct selling industry defies the prophets of doom. Why when the world screams its agony of social injustice and political turmoil, of war and famine, tens of thousands of ordinary Australians have carved for themselves a sanctuary of personal achievement. They have achieved this through their involvement with direct selling, the "can do" people in the people-to-people business.

It is no accident. This industry is built upon the encouragement of people to strive for excellence, to reach for their potential, **to understand that the horizon is not how far you can see but how far you can visualise.**

When Cyndi Kaplan set out to write this book she had no idea that it would lead her to the best kept secret of the decade; to the active, gregarious, self-motivated field force of our 30 Member Companies; to over 400,000 independent, self-employed Australians, mainly women, mostly part-time and supplementing family income. They are of course the life-blood of the industry. Many of them are making this a full-time career, creating successful and substantial distributorships, enchancing and often changing their lifestyles forever.

They in turn are part of the global direct selling fraternity. In 34 countries around the world direct selling associations have been formed. The World Federation of Direct Selling Associations boasts over 1,000 Member Companies, engaging more than 10 million independent sales people and with sales in excess of 50 billion US dollars.

The growth rate in Australia is about 20 per cent per annum. There could be no better time to come into the industry either as a corporation or as an individual to seize the opportunities that are readily available for those with good products and dedication to customer service.

Cyndi's book tells it as it is. The companies, their marketing plans and philosophy, the people, the hard work, the preparation and planning, the striving for excellence, the achievement and rewards, but above all the sheer joy of being part of a vibrant, successful, **expanding industry where recession and depression is excluded from the vocabulary.**

The Beauty of Business will sit proudly alongside Cyndi's great seller **There's a Lipstick in my Briefcase.**

JOHN FULTON

Executive Director, Direct Selling Association of Australia.
Vice Chairman, World Federation of Direct Selling Associations.
August 1992.

PREFACE

What is the Beauty of Business?
A business that gives you the freedom to work
when, where and with whom you choose.
A business that has no glass ceiling and unlimited potential
to earn as much as you desire.
A business that grows through the power of sharing
and the joy of friendship.
A business that has low overheads, minimal start-up costs
and gives free training.
A business that gives you an enviable lifestyle,
a closer family and time for yourself.
A business that not only generates exciting profits, prizes
and travel, but also increases your personal power.

This is the Beauty of Business.

This is the direct selling business.

CHAPTER 1

WHAT DIRECT SELLING CAN DO FOR YOU

WHAT IS DIRECT SELLING?

IT IS THE OPPORTUNITY OF THE NINETIES

There is an explosion of direct selling companies world-wide and Australia is no exception. This is an exciting trend in business today. It is not a fad or a get rich quick scheme.

Although direct selling has been used as a marketing system for more than 30 years, today it is the fastest growing form of retailing. **Because of the difficult economic situation** in the early 1990s, **people are looking for ways to supplement their income.**

Every day news reports on radio, TV and in newspapers contain alarming statistics of **more and more unemployed** and **fewer and fewer jobs**. Australians over-borrowed, over-stretched and over-spent in the eighties. We are now paying the price.

Direct selling allows people to become proactive, to take the initiative and **to do something about their lives** instead of waiting for the economy to improve.

The success of women in developing a direct selling business does much more than keep them personally employed. The more product that is sold, the more product is needed. This stimulates manufacturing and creates further jobs in industry.

Furthermore successful direct selling agents spend more on homes, cars, clothes and accessories and this is what we **need to get the economy moving again**. We need the confidence to spend as well as the confidence to consume, invest and develop new products.

The resounding message I gained through interviewing countless achievers within the direct selling business and the chief executives of the companies themselves, was that the investment in this business was the **investment in developing people**. All companies I spoke to offer training at no or very little cost to the agents. The training is without exception positive, **geared towards growth of the individual** and designed to create more effective human beings. Every female achiever interviewed for this book has emphasised her personal growth as her greatest asset.

Consumers are becoming more conscious of quality of products and value of services. Most direct selling companies produce or distribute a superior **quality product** and provide **personalised service**. This is sadly lacking in the marketplace today.

Direct selling is a method of taking product directly to the consumer via independent sales people who seek out the customer to demonstrate the product usually in the customer's home or business location.

Compare this with traditional retailing where product remains on the shop shelf until found by the customer.

Direct selling is an ideal opportunity for women to establish themselves in business. The central reason for this is that it offers women the possibility of combining their roles of mother, homemaker and business woman. It is possible to operate a direct selling business successfully from home. You can choose your own hours. Start up costs are minimal because there is almost no capital outlay and direct selling offers products that are basic necessities and repeat business.

The **initial costs** vary from company to company. Joining fees are minimal and most starter kits are less than $200.

In the appendix is a description of some of the features you should look for in a company. It highlights the companies, their reputations and track records. It also looks at the marketing plan, philosophy, products and training offered by each company.

Direct sales offers women the opportunity to become financially independent. Even if you have minimal resources, you can join a direct selling company. As a self employed business person you will have control over your own life.

Over 400,000 Australians are now selling direct, via personal referral, through home parties, repeat business and some door to door sales. The sales generated by these people are over **$1 billion. The direct selling business is growing rapidly.** A large percentage of the business is female.

Products cover a large range of cosmetics and skincare, household cleaners, nutritional products, kitchenware, jewellery, toys, books, educational products and clothing.

WHY DIRECT SALES?

This form of selling gives the consumers the opportunity to learn about the product in a relaxed environment before they buy a single item. For example, in the cosmetic area many women buy one jar of product from a department store, another from a pharmacy and use it all together in a haphazard fashion. Direct selling gives women an opportunity to learn about total skin care. Many women do not like to remove their cosmetics in a public place nor do they have time for lengthy consultations in a retail store. **Customers want service and personalised attention.**

BE YOUR OWN BOSS

It is extremely stressful to juggle personal needs, family demands and a full time work schedule in a corporate environment.

In the three years since I published my first book, **There's a Lipstick in my Briefcase**, women have made little further progress into senior positions in corporations or government.

There are still too few women on the boards of Australian companies and too few female politicians. While this is disappointing, many women will have made a conscious choice not to seek these positions. Some women who have pursued corporate careers and achieved great heights have become **disillusioned at the top**. They have admitted defeat, unable to juggle the rigorous demands of work, as well as a satisfactory personal and family life.

While men have traditionally reached their professional goals with the support of women at home, women do not have this privilege. As they say, behind every successful man there's his wife. **Behind every successful woman it's a babysitter and a cleaner.** It's not quite the same.

ADVANTAGES OF HAVING YOUR OWN BUSINESS

Freedom to choose when to work and when to take time for your family is one of the big advantages of being in a home based business. You have flexibility and control over your own time. This is not to say you are likely to work fewer hours, in fact you can expect to put in much more time. But there is a big difference in that you have choice and control over your own life.

Another major advantage of being your own boss is that you are not a victim of decisions made by someone else. You can do what is right for you and your business, and avoid office politics.

If you have spent years at home being available to the needs of others, by establishing your own business you can effectively be less available. They will appreciate you more and take less for granted.

WHEN YOU ARE YOUR OWN BOSS YOU HAVE MORE:

- Flexibility
- Control over your time
- Personal status
- More balanced lifestyle
- Financial rewards
- Personal growth – self-fulfilment

ADVANTAGES OF THE DIRECT SELLING BUSINESS

* No age barrier, educational requirement, sex or nationality bias. It is open to anyone willing to work the business.
* You can set your own hours.
* You have an opportunity to meet people.
* You can keep your present job, if you have one.
* You can choose to work if you don't have a job.
* There are minimal overheads.
* The start up costs are low.
* You get free training and most companies will provide motivational programs.
* You can improve your business and personal skills.
* You can work at your own pace from your own home.

FINANCIAL INDEPENDENCE FOR WOMEN

The illusion of a knight in shining armour taking care of a woman's financial needs has been shattered. At some stage in their lives, many women need to be able to be economically independent and able to support themselves. I strongly believe women must develop their own financial profiles as well as skills for economic survival.

This financial profile entails a woman managing and having in place her own insurance, superannuation, disability cover, savings, emergency cash funds and when possible, investments.

In these times of economic recession, it is often necessary to have two incomes. The irony is **there is no greater risk than having to be dependent upon someone else to provide for you**. You are responsible for your life. You might decide to stay single or through other circumstances need to fend for yourself. This book shows you that you have a choice and how to develop it.

WHY WOMEN ARE WINNERS IN BUSINESS

* Many women work more diligently then men.
* Women often handle problems and people with greater compassion.
* Women often are more practical with money and good at basic budgeting.

- Women think long term in business rather than chase the fast buck.
- Women are determined and often feel the need to prove themselves.
- Most women have an extensive repertoire of skills.

PROFILE OF AN ACHIEVER

The wonderful thing I discovered when interviewing achievers in the direct selling business is that each woman did it in **her own way and with her own style**. Some women had strong charismatic personalities, others displayed incredible persistence and others achieved through their selling and people skills.

There are many creative ways of building a business and you should explore the possibilities to find which style suits your personality. The direct selling business offers women many varied opportunities to **explore their talents, strengths and abilities**. Women who enjoy teaching others build on their teaching skills. Others who are more product orientated emphasise selling. This business has enormous scope for individuals to explore their talents.

REASONS FOR JOINING A DIRECT SELLING COMPANY

The reasons women join direct selling companies vary enormously. Less than 10 per cent of the women involved in the industry choose it as a **full time career**.

- To become financially independent.
- To supplement a wage.
- To supplement the family income.
- To give children a private education.
- For future economic security.
- To make friends.
- To earn money for a special event, trip or project.
- To grow as a person.
- To increase your confidence.

* To build business skills.
* To earn a living as a single person.
* To develop an exciting, stimulating and rewarding career.
* To take the first tentative steps back to the work force after being a homemaker.
* For teachers, nurses, secretaries to earn extra income.
* As a means of purchasing product wholesale.
* To get to know a new area.

"BE IN BUSINESS FOR YOURSELF BUT NOT BY YOURSELF" (Pola motto)

As **Fabian Dattner** said in her book, **Nothing Ventured, Nothing Gained**: "Women's greatest qualities are their ability to network, to nurture, their gentleness, their compassion, their ability to love, their willingness to share information and their keenness to see others succeed".

These characteristics are increasingly perceived as the qualities of the modern leader. Today more women will succeed by using their innate abilities. Women do not need to compete with others. They can achieve on their own terms.

My first book was a guide for female entrepreneurs. After speaking to women in many different cities, towns and countries, I realised some women were not the pioneering type. There were some who had brilliant ideas and the drive, stamina and resources to develop these ideas. There were many others who wanted to be **part of an organisation**, who needed to belong. There were others who were **great team** players and did not want to set up business alone.

Direct selling companies provide opportunities for women who want the benefits of their own businesses, independence as well as the support, product and training of a larger company.

The women who succeed and reach the top in direct sales enjoy the same status, privileges and financial rewards as independent business entrepreneurs or proprietors of small business.

THE FUTURE OF WOMEN IN DIRECT SELLING

WOMEN ARE IDEALLY SUITED TO THE INDUSTRY OF DIRECT SALES

- Direct sales appeals to the lifestyle needs of women.
- Women today want more balance in their lives.
- Many are frustrated by the lack of opportunity for executive status in large corporations.
- They are still not equally rewarded at corporate level.
- Direct selling is fundamentally a business centred around the ability to communicate, share and involve others.
- Women respond well to a business environment with a win-win approach.
- And they are keen to see everyone winning.
- Women have a willingness to share information.
- Women are natural nurturers.
- Women are good team leaders.
- They are excellent with detail.
- Women use their intuition in business.
- Women have well developed communication skills.
- Women are used to networking on a personal level.

Up to now women have always had to be twice as good as men to be accepted in a male dominated corporate business world. In the direct selling industry **rewards are based solely on performance**. Women can shine without limits, boundaries or politics preventing achievement.

Most of the product ranges in direct sales are **highly consumable**. The products which range from cosmetics and household goods to nutritional and health foods, toys and jewellery are usually bought by women. It is women who budget for the items and who make decisions about where, when and how they will be acquired.

Women often have zigzag careers. Some women might start working when they become mothers and want to earn some extra money. As the family structure changes they gradually have more time available to devote to careers. Other women start work well before having children. **Jobs such as secretaries, clerks and teachers have limited prospects.**

Direct sales provide the opportunity for both earning money part time and building an interesting, stimulating and challenging career. The choice and flexibility is available depending on the needs of the individual.

CHAPTER 2

GUIDELINES FOR SELECTING A COMPANY

Introduction

List of Companies Reviewed

Points to Consider

An Opportunity for Women

Choose One

INTRODUCTION

A list of 15 companies that belong to the Direct Selling Association of Australia can be found in the Appendix. I have covered the history of each company, a product description, its marketing plan, training, philosophy, rewards and incentives. I have not attempted to give details, analyse or compare the commission and remuneration given by each company. This is because I think everyone needs to look at the broader picture and to consider whether or not the company and/or its product will suit them rather than how much money they will make.

WHAT IS NETWORK MARKETING

According to Kearney and Bandley, the authors of **Network Marketing:** "Network marketing is a legal, direct sales plan which moves product from the manufacturer through multiple levels of distributors to an end consumer who pays the retail price for the product. Since each distributor is an independent contractor, she buys direct, pays a wholesale price, and then sets the sales price generally in line with the company's suggested retail price. You must have retail customers for your product. You must sell your product in order to receive commission on product moving through other parts of your organisation."

ILLEGAL PYRAMID SCHEMES

As Kearney and Bandley have stated, "Pyramid schemes in which those sponsored would pay a large sum of money for a position in the network has been declared illegal". It is illegal for a company to pay a fee for recruiting.

All companies interviewed for this book belong to the Direct Selling Association and conduct their business according to legitimate marketing practices.

GET RICH QUICK SCHEMES

If anybody suggests to you a "get rich quick" scheme where you will not have to sell product as a basis of the business, you should be suspicious of their offer.

This is not an overnight business. Like any business it takes consistent time, effort and application to develop the business. There are no short cuts and building a network needs considerable hard work and long hours. If you are lured into a program and offered a life style of freedom and lazing next to a pool sipping Martinis hoping that the dollars will roll in, think again.

You do have freedom to choose when, where and how you work. Freedom to do no work results in no business activity and no money. When you have successfully established a large network you will reap the benefits of your time invested in **teaching and training others.** At that point you will earn commissions on their activities. The pot of gold will be yours only if you **teach others to do what you do.**

LIST OF COMPANIES REVIEWED

Aloette	**Le Reve**
Amway	**Mary Kay**
Avon	**Mini Minor**
Avroy Shlain	**Nature's Sunshine**
Beauty For All Seasons	**Neways**
Billicart	**Nu Skin**
Elmon	**Nutri-Metics**
Emma Page	**One Earth**
Encyclopaedia Britannica	**Pola**
Fensmore	**Pro-Ma**
Forever Living	**Rawleigh**
Herbalife	**Reliv**
Jigsaw	**Undercover Underwear**
Lady Remington	**World Book**
Learner's World	

POINTS TO CONSIDER

EXAMINE THE COMPANY

- Is there a good management team?
- Is there a good compensation plan for the distributors?
- Are there well designed sales brochures and literature?
- Do they have an efficient dispatch system?
- What is the turn around from receipt of order to dispatch? This will affect your sales.
- What is the growth potential of the company?
- Visit the head office or distribution centre if you are in the same city.

EXAMINE THE PRODUCT

- Are the products consumable?
- How often could you service the customer for reorders?
- Is the price of the product competitive?
- Do the products offer value and quality?
- Is there a large range of products?
- Who do the products appeal to – men, women, children or the whole family?
- What are the company's future plans regarding product research?
- Is consumer satisfaction guaranteed?
- How big is the range of products?
- What is the competition with regard to products?

THE START-UP COSTS

- Ensure there is no inventory requirement other than an initial kit at a set price, when you become a distributor.
- What is the cost of the start up kit? Sales kits should be sold at actual cost to the new distributor.

EXAMINE THE INCENTIVES, REWARDS AND TRAINING PROGRAM

- What incentives or prizes does the company offer?
- Does the company provide a maintained car?
- If so at what level is this achievable?
- Does the company offer ongoing training?

* Does the company pay for you to attend national conventions or seminars? If not, can you earn your way there?
* Is there a good program of training and material for you to use when training?
* What are the incentives – car, overseas travel, cash prizes?

EXAMINE THE MARKETING PLAN

Ensure that the focus of any marketing program **is to promote retail sales** to non-participants. Many companies recognise purchases for personal or family use in reasonable amounts are also retail sales. As Bob Quinn has said in his article in **Personal Success** (July 1992): "You can have the best marketing plan in the industry but without products that people need, buy and continue to re-order, success will be difficult to achieve". **Retail sales are the bottom line in direct selling.**

The more money you wish the harder and longer you have to work to create a sales organisation. You need a stable long term plan in order to achieve regular income. For example, if you want to earn $5,000 per month you would need to personally sponsor 100 people who pursue an active business. You could realistically develop this level in between 18 months to two years. It would depend whether you wanted to build your business around retailing product or sponsoring other people into the business or a combination of both.

EXAMINE THE COMMISSION STRUCTURE

In the direct selling business you will build a sales team and receive commissions on that team's monthly sales performance.
- Sales commissions should not be paid for the mere act of sponsoring other distributors. Commission should only be paid as a result of selling product to a consumer. This ensures that illegal pyramid schemes will not occur.
- Find out when commissions are paid.
- Make sure there are computer generated records.
- Are income projections offered by the person who sponsors you realistic?
- Who pays bonuses to your team, you or the company?
- At what point do you pay for the products purchased?
- How does the company structure its bonus payments?

EXAMINE THE PHILOSOPHY

Make sure you are comfortable with the philosophy and beliefs of the company you select. Choose a product you will enjoy selling. For example, if you like jewellery you will probably choose Emma Page, if you adore children, Jigsaw is an obvious choice. Women interested in cosmetics, beauty and helping other women look better will gravitate towards a cosmetic company. An interest in health and nutrition will take you to explore one of the nutritional food ranges.

It is of no value to flit from one company to another. Once you have done your research make a decision and make a commitment. I have seen "direct selling junkies" who never succeed because they keep moving from one company to another hoping the grass is greener in the other company.

LOYALTY

I strongly believe the amount you make through direct selling depends on your personal commitment, your love and passion for selling the product, your desire to teach and share the opportunity with others. The money you make does not depend on the fact that one company might offer a few more percent than another. Every achiever told me their company had the best product and the best marketing plan.

DIRECT SELLING ASSOCIATION OF AUSTRALIA

All companies reviewed in this book are members of the Direct Selling Association of Australia Inc. (DSAA). They carry out their business according to an approved code of ethics and business practices. I found all products to be of high quality and the level of administrative efficiency in each company was excellent. Most leading consultants interviewed remarked on the high level of support they received from their head offices.

AN OPPORTUNITY FOR WOMEN

Most companies had a very high percentage of female consultants. The only exception was Encyclopaedia Britannica which is 75 per cent male dominated. The companies which distribute a broader product range like Amway and Dominant, as well as nutritional companies like Neo-Life, Advanced Life Foods and Herbalife have equal numbers of men and women. The cosmetic companies are made up of 95 per cent women.

However, as women develop their businesses to a higher level, many partners or husbands join their wives in the business. Many senior regional directors at Nutri-Metics have their husbands as full time business partners. Pro-Ma also encourages husband and wife teams. This is made easier through the company's product range for men.

The direct selling industry **is growing at a rate of 20-25 per cent per year** in times when most other businesses are experiencing negative growth. This reflects an ever growing opportunity for women to develop careers in an industry which both rewards and recognises achievement without discrimination.

AN OPPORTUNITY FOR MIGRANT WOMEN

From my own experience as an immigrant to Australia, I am aware of the difficulties most migrant women face when changing countries. **Often language and culture is a huge barrier.** Many talented and skilled women are forced to do menial, low paid jobs in which they cannot use their qualifications. **The direct selling industry offers these people an equal opportunity.** They are able to network and establish businesses without restraint. The industry also offers great potential for social benefits, integration and the development of communication skills across cultures.

CHOOSE ONE COMPANY

Once you have been through all the selection criteria, make a commitment. If you stop and start in a number of different companies you will not only confuse yourself but lose credibility with the people you approach as customers. If you are selling cosmetics one week and jewellery or vitamins the next, your can't expect your customers to take you seriously. Spend time doing your research thoroughly. Once you have made up your mind which company to join stick to your decision. **Don't become a direct selling junkie.**

The amount of money you make is not dependent on whether one company offers a few per cent more commission than another initially. It is the whole picture which contributes to building a successful business.

CHAPTER 3

THE KITCHEN TABLE BUSINESS

How to Plan Your Business

Develop Your Own Financial Profile

Coping with a Home Work Schedule

How to set up Your Business at Home

HOW TO PLAN YOUR BUSINESS

LOW CAPITAL OUTLAY

The attraction of many woman to the direct selling business is the low start up cost. You can start business in this industry with a minimal investment. With as little as $50 to $200 you can buy a kit, join a company as a consultant and start selling, promoting and recruiting a team.

Your major outlay is **your time and effort.** You learn to put a value on these qualities. In the direct selling business you can earn or save money in most companies through four areas.

- Commissions.
- Bonuses on your team sales.
- Discounts on products.
- Tax deductions.

The objective is to combine and maximise each of these areas. You might also decide to do more selling or recruiting or balance the two.

BUDGETING

In order to run your own business effectively you need to anticipate your expenses, monitor purchases and control your cash flow. Bear in mind it might take up to a year of full time activity before you can rely on direct sales for your livelihood. Most companies advocate you earn twice your present salary in commissions before you go full time.

EXPENSES INCURRED IN RUNNING A BUSINESS

*	Postage	*	Petrol
*	Stationery	*	Facsimile (optional)
*	Leases	*	Copying
*	Telephone	*	Cleaning service
*	Insurances	*	Travel
*	Rent (partial)	*	Car expenses

You often have to spend money to make money. To build your team you might decide to travel to another city or town. The investment will be yours, but so will the business expansion.

Make a list of your anticipated monthly expenses as well as some unexpected payments. If you are relying on your income for total support you need to create a budget for your **personal expenses** as well.

PERSONAL EXPENSES

• Rent	• Clothing	• Education
• Gifts	• Holidays	• Medical
• Food	• Entertainment	• Pocket money for kids
• Household maintenance, water		• Electricity

Work out how much you need to earn each month, set your goals and adjust your level of activity to meet them. **Remember in this business the only limits are the limits you set yourself.** The time and effort you expend are your choice. The more productive activity you generate the more you earn. Your income is in your own hands.

OPERATE A SEPARATE BANK ACCOUNT FOR YOUR BUSINESS

Set up a separate bank account. Don't keep personal and business monies together in the same account. It makes it more complicated later on to account for certain expenditures. Use your business account for expenses that are claimable as legitimate business expenses.

TAXATION BENEFITS

If you own a legitimate business you will be able to make claims for:

* Business travel (air, hotel, taxis)	* Car repairs
* Rent (office, storage)	* Car payments
* Telephone	* Car registration
* Office cleaning	* Car insurance
* Stationery	* Insurance
* Postage	* Electricity
* Fax lease payments	* Office furniture
* Copier (optional)	* Training books, tapes
* Petrol	and seminars

DEVELOPING YOUR OWN FINANCIAL PROFILE

Once you can support yourself you will be able to create a lifestyle you enjoy. After you have put some resources away in savings, you can start to be creative with your cash.

- A savings plan – superannuation.
- Stocks and shares.
- Government bonds.
- Cash savings you have access to on a daily basis.
- Fixed deposits you do not touch.
- Aim to save $10,000 which you could put in a high interest fixed deposit account. Reinvest the interest or splurge on a treat.
- Purchase your own home and repay as much of the mortgage as possible.
- Purchase an investment property you can negatively gear.

COPING WITH A HOME WORK SCHEDULE

FEELING ISOLATED

Isolation can be a major problem for many people used to working in an office, retail business or factory. Gone is the friendly work environment and the comfort of having co-workers around you. Gone is the boss you could turn to for advice and who had to bear the responsibility for any mistakes.

When you go full time into direct sales you are on your own except for the time you spend servicing customers, going to training sessions and holding parties and demonstrations.

WAYS OF OVERCOMING ISOLATION

The need for social contact becomes more acute when you work alone at home. Create a balance for yourself each week between times you spend alone at your desk and time you spend networking, recruiting and seeing customers.

Set aside time to talk to customers and potential customers by telephone and making personal visits to service them. Use lunchtime to do errands to the post office and bank. Quick short chats with your friends will keep you in touch.

Maintain contact with trade and professional organisations. Women's executive groups are useful for networking. Set time aside to go to lectures, networking meetings, seminars, conferences, workshops and other informative gatherings. At these meetings you can improve your business skills, get stimulated and make many contacts, meet potential clients and customers. (See Appendix for a list of useful networks.)

PITFALLS OF WORKING FROM HOME

Running a business from home can be successful, satisfying and fun. It eliminates commuting to an office and has many advantages around the flexibility of hours. However these advantages can turn into disadvantages. Here are some of the problems.

- Interruptions from telephone or neighbours.
- Educating family and friends about your business hours.
- Coping with small children and a home business.
- Motivating yourself and maintaining faith in your abilities.
- Procrastination.
- Coping with house work.
- Being able to switch off after hours.
- Learning to be a self-starter instead of waiting for a boss to tell you what to do.
- Feeling isolated.

COPING WITH INTERRUPTIONS

The telephone is the life blood of your business. It can also create many interruptions and waste a great deal of your time. When friends call you for a chat in the time you have set aside for work be firm and arrange to call back. This is where a separate line would come in very useful. As soon as you can afford it have a separate telephone line installed for your business.

Managing your time becomes crucial if you want to combine the benefits of working at home with your other roles. I have dealt with this is detail in the chapter on time management.

FAMILY SUPPORT

Your family have to get used to you working at home instead of going out to work. They might even have to adapt to you working at home instead of being a full time housewife. In the chapter on **Juggling Roles** I explain this more fully. Set yourself specific work time and time to be with your family. Create your own structure.

DOMESTIC BLISS

You have to find ways to manage the household when you start a business at home. Recognise there is no such thing as **superwoman.** In the early days of setting up your business at home you become more aware of all the imperfections. Dust, untidy cupboards and tarnished silver will all seem to need immediate attention. **Remember domestic chores will not develop your business.** Find ways to make your home run more efficiently.

*   Reduce shopping to once a week.
*   Tolerate an imperfect house, perfectionism is time consuming.
*   Organise the family to help with chores.
*   Get household appliances that save you money.
*   Get a cleaning service.

DISPLAYING PRODUCTS

Create a display in your office of the products you work with. Keep sales materials and some promotional flyers and product catalogues close by. This will have a positive effect on your daily activities and strengthen your commitment to your product line.

HOW TO SET UP YOUR BUSINESS AT HOME

Every business needs an office, whether it's a desk in the corner of a family room or kitchen or a separate study. It is practical to have a desk you don't need to clear away. You need to be able to set yourself up and not have to move. It is very frustrating to have to keep resetting up your office. Psychologically you need a space, however small that totally belongs to your business activities.

The layout of your office is crucial to your comfort and efficiency. Spend a little time planning the placement of your equipment and furniture. Efficient storage is an essential feature in a well organised home office.

OFFICE FURNITURE

There is no need to buy expensive new furniture when you first start your business at home. It is easy to acquire second hand desks and chairs. Take into account natural lighting, storage, telephone outlets and power points. Once you have taken note of the practical aspects of setting up an office by acquiring a desk, chair and shelves, create an environment in which you feel secure, happy and at peace. Surround yourself with paintings, posters, plants or books that make you feel at ease.

Make sure all the practical objects are at arms length so you don't have to keep getting up and moving around while you work.

OFFICE ESSENTIALS

Equipment
- Telephone.
- Answering machine.
- Facsimile machine – hard to do without.
- Personal computer – optional.
- Tape recorder/radio – soft music in the background is conducive to concentrating.
- Desk trays – in and out.
- Alphabetical file for correspondence.
- Box with an indexed customer card system.

Furniture
- Desk – large and roomy, with drawers.
- Comfortable desk chair.
- Heater.
- Good lighting – desk lamp.
- Bookshelves – packed with motivational books, company manual, reference books.

Personal items
- Business card holder.
- Pinboard – invitations, events, inspirational sayings, photographs and postcards of your favourite places.
- Mug – your own special one.
- Jar – pencils, pens, ruler.
- Waste-paper basket.
- White out, stapler, scissors, sticky tape, paperclips, highlighter, address book, calculator.
- Photographs of family and friends.

Stationery
- Diary – large, one page per day, for party dates, client orders, goals, events, conferences.
- Deposit book for business accounts.
- Business cards.

- Compliment slips.
- Envelopes.
- Copy paper.
- Self adhesive address labels with your name, address and phone number on label.

COMPUTERS

Personal computers play an important role in business today. Used properly, they can make your home office more efficient and easy to run. This is not essential until your business has grown to considerable size.

There are many different brands of personal computers available, but basically they can be divided into two groups, the IBM-compatible family and the Apple Macintosh family. For most home businesses, an IBM compatible PC will be the cheapest, both in terms of hardware (the actual computer, keyboard, monitor, mouse and so on) and software (the programs that make the computer operate as a word-processor and database for accounts etc).

Clearly, buying your equipment is only the first step. It will pay you to enrol in a course which will teach you how to get the most out of the equipment you are purchasing. Often these courses are provided by the computer company or you may prefer to do one of the many courses run by community colleges.

PHOTOCOPIER

A photocopier is a very useful office tool. Before rushing off to buy one see if you can use one at your local library or print shop where you pay per copy. If you find you do need your own copier, it is worth looking around for reconditioned models which often come with a guarantee and service contract. Remember there are more costs involved with a photocopier than just the purchase price. You need to buy toner and paper and will probably need a service contract which costs you a certain amount for every copy made.

FACSIMILE

Depending on your business, a facsimile machine can be a great asset. You will find it pays for itself very soon in the additional work it generates and the money and time it saves in courier and postal charges. You need to weigh up your needs. If you have any doubts, use the services of a fax bureau or post office for a while to see whether the volume of faxes justifies getting your own machine.

My facsimile machine is my best friend. I have had it for more than five years and it has been the greatest business asset I have ever acquired. I bought my fax in the days when they cost about $5,000. Now you can pick up a good second hand one for around $500. Faxes are time and cost savers. They are much more efficient than a phone call.

They enable you to communicate precise information to the appropriate person at any time of the day or night. Phone calls usually take longer and most people still want written confirmation of a call. In this business the fax can be an excellent link with head office and other distributors especially if your team is scattered across the country.

TELEPHONES

The telephone is a vital instrument for the direct selling business. First make sure your customers can find your telephone number in the directory. If you can afford the cost, it is best to have a separate business telephone line installed immediately and listed in the private subscribers and in the business (yellow pages) telephone directories.

Nothing creates a worse impression with clients than an unanswered business telephone. It is not a good idea to let your young children answer the telephone. This gives the impression of, at best, a part-time business which is not being run professionally. Older children, on the other hand, can be an asset if they are taught to answer the phone properly.

ANSWERING MACHINES

You will need to invest in a reliable telephone answering machine to attend to calls when you are not physically there to answer the phone. There will be times too when you do not wish to be interrupted for instance during a client meeting.

MOBILE TELEPHONE

Another more expensive way of handling calls when you are not physically in the office is to invest in a mobile telephone. This is ideal if you spend much time away from the office. You could list both your office number and your mobile number in the telephone directory. Your answering machine could advise callers to try your mobile number.

SET UP YOUR RECORDS

When working from home there is a greater need to keep separate and efficient track records of every activity and transaction. Keep a receipt book, a cash book and a deposit book with full details of each deposit. Keep a running list of monthly business expenses. If you do this on a monthly basis it prevents a great build up of paper work. It also makes your annual tax return a simple procedure. I keep an envelope for all loose receipts, cash dockets and credit card slips. Each month I seal the envelope, write the month's name and keep it for my tax return.

CREDITORS' FILE

Keep a creditors' file and alphabetically file all accounts, invoices and statements. Once a month, go through your expenses and write out cheques. This will make it easy to keep track of your cash flow.

INSURANCE

Find a reliable insurance agent. Find out what policies you need to cover your equipment: copier, fax, answer machine, computer and desks. It is also worthwhile to have disability insurance in case of illness. For women today, there are policies covering many health problems including breast cancer. Research your personal needs and take out adequate cover.

CHAPTER 4

THE SECRET OF SELF-ESTEEM

THE SECRET OF SELF-ESTEEM

My favourite song is Whitney Houston's **The Greatest Love of All** which is about loving ourselves. Self love is the basis of a healthy personality. Many of us are plagued with negative thoughts about ourselves. We are our own worst enemies. We need to learn how to become our own **best friend**. If we treated ourselves with as much care, generosity and tolerance as we would a special friend, we would experience self love.

As Mary Kay says: "Women need to reverse the Golden Rule on themselves. Do unto yourself as you would unto others. **Be kind to yourself.**"

It is our basic right to be happy and to create a worthwhile life for ourselves. We have the right to feel and we need to respect our own feelings. We need to value our bodies, our time and the special qualities that make us unique. Addictive and destructive behaviour such as drug abuse, alcoholism and obesity stems from basic lack of self-esteem.

TREAT YOURSELF AS YOU WOULD A SPECIAL FRIEND

* Trust your own feelings.
* Value yourself and your time.
* Treat yourself with compassion, care and respect.
* Believe in your own special qualities.
* Value your body.
* Don't put yourself down.
* Never say: "I'm hopeless", "I'm sorry", or "I'm not good at".
* Use "I" to ask for what you want and need.

CONFIDENCE

The outward manifestation of self-esteem is self-confidence. Who is this confident woman? Was she born with bags of confidence? Is she just lucky? Can you build your confidence? How do you go about getting it if you don't have it?

After speaking to thousands of women across Australia I experienced a number of similar reactions. Many of them came up to me after my presentation and said, "It's easy for you. **You are loaded with confidence**". I confessed that just the opposite was true. When I started my business I was 24 and a mother of two young children. I was shy, reserved and unsure of my identity, my femininity or my own potential. I faced rejection and setbacks. I went back and tried again and again. Eventually I tasted a small measure of success. **These small steps of success started to build a ladder of confidence.** With each step forward something deep inside me began to crystallise; the magic quality of self confidence.

HOW A CONFIDENT WOMAN BEHAVES

- She loves herself.
- She knows what she wants.
- She understands herself.
- She thinks positively.
- She feels powerful and feminine.
- She does not set herself up to be perfect.
- She is lively and energetic.
- She is peaceful, relaxed and calm.
- She solves problems creatively.
- We feel secure with her because we know where we stand – she is not sending out any double messages.
- Confident women continually adapt and change according to new and varying situations. They are flexible and not judgemental.

WHAT ARE YOUR VALUES

One of the greatest signs of lack of confidence is a persistent difficulty in making decisions. Sometimes this difficulty is revealed in anxiety, procrastination and feelings of insecurity.

In order to feel strong in ourselves we need to have our own personal set of values by which we lead our lives. These form the basic framework of our lives. They could originate in a religion or form part of a cultural heritage. When people embark on a personal developmental course they become aware of how muddled their own philosophy of life is. Often their values are at war with each other.

If we want to feel truly confident we **need to define what our values really are.** We need to break the habit of trying to please everyone all of the time. Once we have our priorities and our values in place they act as a guide for our decision making.

UNDERSTANDING YOUR HISTORY

Much of our lack of confidence can be traced back to our childhood and other important formative experiences. My parents brought me up to believe I was special, well-loved and capable of doing anything. This basic belief has been very valuable. I was taught to believe in myself. It gave me the capacity to take on new challenges and trust that I could achieve my goals.

If we look back and **understand influences in our childhood**, we can attain awareness and insight. There is no point in blaming our parents, our past mistakes and other people for where we are now. But we can understand these events and influences and use the knowledge as a spring board to a healthy self esteem. Babies are born confident. We need to regain our innate self confidence.

ANALYSE YOURSELF

Many women underestimate themselves. Draw up a list of your assets using the following guidelines.
*   What are your talents?
*   What are your skills?
*   What experience have you had?
*   What are your strengths as a person?

TAKE RESPONSIBILITY FOR YOURSELF

"If it's to be it's up to me."
You are the only person who can change your behaviour. No one can make you happy. You need to accept responsibility for your own circumstances. So often we say, "If only I were more intelligent/rich/beautiful/married to someone else....."

Highly successful people recognise responsibility. They do not blame circumstances, conditions, other people, their parents or their past for their behaviour. **It's not what happens to us that counts but how we handle what happens to us.** We are inspired by people who maintain magnificent emotional strength in the face of problems. We must learn to act, rather than be acted upon. Focus your energy on areas you can change.

The road to confidence is open for all of us to travel, embrace and enjoy. **Tell yourself every day that you are:**

SPECIAL AND WONDERFUL
LOVED AND LOVABLE

PARIS PASSION

Ten years ago I went on my first international business trip. My motivation for the trip was to diversify my product range and expand my business. **I had a great ulterior motive to galvanise me into action.** My dream was to spend my 30th birthday drinking champagne with my best girlfriend who was a journalist in New York.

Once I had a reason to go, the trip took on a life of its own. My first exposure to an international toy fair was in Nuremburg, Germany. It is the biggest annual toy fair in the world. There were over 20 halls the size of the Sydney Entertainment Centre filled with 6,000 exhibitions and 80,000 delegates from every corner of the globe. I was stimulated, fascinated and exhilarated that a little home cottage business in my garage could get me to an international toy fair.

I was completely bedazzled, bewildered and confused by the huge array of products I saw. I met up with two buyers from back home. They suggested I join them for a weekend in Paris which seemed a preposterous idea at the time.

There was no way I could leave the fair after one day and disappear to Paris. It would take me at least a week to fully examine all the stands of merchandise at Nuremburg.

But a few hours later, feeling even more foot sore, bewildered and over-stimulated I started to fantasise about this weekend in Paris. I had always wanted to go to Paris and soon the vision was overwhelmingly compelling.

I arrived in Paris on the stroke of midnight wearing jeans, a fur coat and carrying not much more than my toothbrush. I gave the name of the hotel my friends had given me to the cab driver. I found myself at an extraordinary, elegant hotel situated on the Champs Elysée. This was way out of my league. At the time my husband was a fifth year medical student and we were living on sausages and mash.

As I arrived I saw the buyers standing at the desk. When they saw me their faces lit up and they announced they were waiting for me to go to the Moulin Rouge. At that point there was no way I could lose face. As I said, **"You have to fake it till you make it"**.

In my coolest and most sophisticated voice I asked for a room for the weekend. My room looked like a version of Marie Antoinette's and was decorated accordingly. The weekend cost me more than $1000. I had the best weekend of my life. It took me over six months to pay off the credit card and moreover, I did not tell my husband what I had done until seven years later.

I decided however, that this weekend was a great investment in my own psyche. I realised after that experience that no knight in shining armour was going to come and give me gorgeous, glamorous, weekends in Paris. **"If it was to be, it would be up to me."**

I made a resolution then and there to expand the vision I had for my business. I did not only want a business that was locally based. I wanted an international business. I wanted to import from different countries. I wanted to export and I wanted to develop my business on an international level. This was a wonderful example of how an experience motivated me to expand, change and develop the business.

From then on my business became the vehicle for much exciting international travel where I met interesting and stimulating people who shared the same ideas and goals. Whenever days seem particularly mundane, tedious or stressful, I have this wonderful warm memory of my weekend in Paris tucked away in the back of my mind to draw on, to savour and to enjoy over and over again.

We all have options and choices in our lives if we are prepared to explore them. Many of us are stuck in a rut or dead end situation because we won't allow ourselves to take advantage of new opportunities. If you keep doing what you are doing now, you'll be in the same place this time next year. Nothing in your life can change unless you change your own responses and behaviour.

WHAT DO WOMEN REALLY WANT?

Recently I went to a stimulating lecture given by an American marketing consultant entitled "**What do women really want?**". The lecturer said **women today are moving targets**, one day an executive, the next a traditional housewife and mother. In one day a woman is a combination of so many roles. I asked my 15 year old daughter, Nikki, "What do women really want?". She said, "Mum it's simple. Women want to be beautiful. They want to have a gorgeous body, to smell wonderful and to have men love and adore them." Here I was for 15 years, blazing the trail as an entrepreneurial woman and she put it all in a nutshell for me.

I believe women want all that but they also want another dimension to their lives. **They want to fulfil themselves** through work, a profession or a business in which they can express their talents, stretch themselves and to find satisfaction and financial independence.

RESPECT YOUR FEELINGS

Feelings rarely lie. Feelings are the barometer of what is going on for us. Listen to the body sensations that tell you what emotions you are experiencing. **Learn to decipher your feelings.** Tensions in your body, a nervous tummy or migraines are signals something is not harmonious in your life. Find an appropriate way of expressing your feelings. Suppressed emotions are a drain on your energy and a major factor in contributing to a lower self-esteem, lack of confidence and depression. Examine the cause and reasons for your feelings and try to deal with the root of it.

ALTER YOUR LIFESTYLE

Examine your lifestyle and try and find out whether you:
- Are living according to your values?
- Have the right balance between work and play?
- Have the kind of relationships you want?
- Are happy with your work or career?

Women also want a balance in their lives between their relationships, work, family, home and their own needs. **Essentially women like to operate from a base of inner harmony and spiritual integrity.** Many women in the work force are feeling stretched, splintered and scattered. Their energy is being dissipated and fragmented.

As **Susan Faludi** said in her new book **Backlash**, "Women may be free and equal but they have never been more miserable". The status of women has never been higher but their emotional state has never been lower. The feminist myth of independence has turned this generation of women into unloved and unhappy people. Women want to love and be loved. But they don't want to give up their career and economic independence to achieve this.

The direct selling business gives women an opportunity to do both.

WHAT IS HAPPINESS?

We can therefore assume that happiness for most women would be HAVING IT ALL: husband, home, children, career and time for themselves. Women do not want to live on a frenetic merry-go-round. Most women do not want to leave little children for eight to ten hours per day in child care. We know we can have it all but not all at the same time. When children are little we need to invest more time in them. Take the time to know what you want and take action to achieve your goals.

MAKE SUCCESS A HABIT

We are not all born successful but we can learn from successful and effective people how to do it better. Success depends on a combination of right attitudes, motivation, effective behaviour and a little bit **of magic and faith.**

WHEN ARE YOU A SUCCESS

Enjoy the journey. To an extent I can think of myself as a success today because I have achieved many of my past goals. However, **there is never a final goal.** You never get there. That's the fun of it. There is always a new goal to accomplish and new challenges. **Success is a process,** a way of living.

INGREDIENTS FOR SUCCESS

* **Motivation – You have to want to do it.** It might be through a desire for money, freedom, status, flexible life style or independence. You must want to be a winner to succeed. All the right techniques and ingredients won't get you to the winning line without an inner need for achievement. As Pablo Picasso said: **"It is your work in life that is the ultimate seduction".** For all those who succeed, however difficult the road, not to have done it would have been more difficult.

* **Self-esteem** – Love yourself, enjoy your own company. Put value on your time, effort and energy.

* **Self-confidence** – Believe in yourself, trust yourself. **"Fake it 'til you make it",** act confident until you feel it inside.

* **Belief in yourself** – Believe that you deserve success. Believe you have the talents and skills to achieve.

* **Integrity** – This ensures you will be in business for a long time. Do business with the idea you will develop honest, ongoing relationships with customers. Look for win-win opportunities in your dealings.

* **Vision** – You need to have a dream that drives you. **A goal is a dream in action.** Visualise your goals and this will subconsciously act as a powerful motivator. **You can't get lost if you know where you are going.**

* **Take initiative** – be proactive. Nothing happens in your own business unless you make it happen. Learn to be captain of your ship, master of your destiny.

* **Planning and preparation** – Make sure you plan and acquire the knowledge, skills and assistance you need.

* **Commitment** – When you make a commitment to a project things start to happen. Stick with an idea to the end.

* **Determination and hard work** – You need to do whatever you have to do to achieve success.

* **Persistence** – Have staying power. Never take **no** for an answer. Always stay with it. As Churchill said: **"Never, never, never give up."**

* **Resourceful** – You need to find creative ways to solve problems. **Do more with less.** Use resources more economically. Business is a matter of solving problems. When the problems stop, business stops. You need to have common sense to solve problems with minimum time, energy and expenditure. You need to be flexible in your approaches because if you become obsessed with one idea it might block your ability to see another solution.

* **Creativity** – Women are especially creative. Use lateral thinking to come up with innovative solutions. Think of alternative ways to do things.

* **Discipline** – A successful business does not happen without consistent effort. We need to invest regular time, effort and resources.
* **Keep learning** – You need to keep reading, learning new skills and finding better ways of developing your business. Stay open, aware and receptive.
* **Knowledge** – In order to succeed you need **product knowledge.** You need to **understand people** and you need to know what is happening in your business.
* **Ability to lead, delegate and motivate others.**
* **Ability to take risks** – Without being a gambler, you need to take risks to develop your business. You need a sense of adventure and you need to take responsibility for your actions if things don't work out.
* **Enthusiasm** – With this quality you can draw people to you. It is a very contagious quality. It attracts like a magnet.
* **Love What You Do and the money will follow.** I believe money itself doesn't amount to success. Choose work you love and products you enjoy and the money will follow.
* **Energy** – You need energy to achieve great goals. Energy is a by-product of loving your work, being enthusiastic and having the desire to achieve.
* **Bounce back** – You need to pick yourself up and start again. Being in business is like being in a boxing ring. Sometimes the punches come from all directions. You have to be able to handle the blows and bounce back.
* **Luck** – You make your own luck. Through action, effort and the process of doing, you get lucky.
* **Sense of humour** – Ability to laugh at yourself, ability to have fun.

THE COMPETITIVE SPIRIT

"Competition can be a very strong motivation. I have learned that it becomes most powerful when you compete with yourself and when you learn from your failures," says Mary Kay.

As I progressed through my own career, my competitive spirit encouraged and helped me through some very difficult times. With each new challenge I concentrated on competing with myself. Each month I calculated my sales and I always wanted my earnings to be a little more than the month before. Whatever it needed to create the increased sales, I was prepared to do it. **The beauty of direct selling is the opportunity it gives each woman to compete with herself.** To improve your own personal best and become as successful as you want.

I believe you can have anything you want as long as you are prepared to pay the price for it. Competing and striving to excel can also be a lot of fun. It creates a self imposed pressure and urgency.

WAYS TO ENHANCE YOUR SELF-ESTEEM

- Take full responsibility for your life. Don't be a martyr.
- Stop blaming others. Don't see yourself as a victim.
- Consciously generate positive thoughts and feelings.
- Associate with others who make you feel good about yourself.
- Do as many as you can of the activities you love.
- Stop being critical of yourself. Practice self-forgiveness.
- Treat yourself as you would a special friend.
- Don't try to change others. Change your own behaviour.
- Live in the present. Don't waste time regretting the past. Move on.
- Stop feeling guilty. It is a negative emotion.
- Learn from your mistakes. Don't regret them.
- Keep a diary of all your achievements big and small.
- Invest money in your personal growth. Expose yourself to stimulating speakers, motivational books and tapes. Keep learning.
- Schedule time for yourself.
- Don't compare yourself with others. Compete with yourself.
- Always have something to look forward to.
- Express your feelings, respect the feeling of others.
- Live with a sense of integrity. Be true to yourself.
- **Be willing to laugh at yourself**, at life and with others. Laughter is still the best medicine. Develop a sense of humour, have fun with what you do. **Don't take yourself too seriously.**
- Live every day **FULLY** as if it were your last.

CHAPTER 5

BUILDING DREAMS

Goal Setting for Success

Why Set Goals?

Goal Setting Techniques

Cover all Areas of Your Life

Creative Visualisation

The Power of Intent

GOAL SETTING FOR SUCCESS

G oal setting is fun, rewarding and achieves results. **A goal is a dream in action.** It is a simple, easy process that you can practice at any level in your life. It influences your being, doing and having options in life. Life's options include being happy, healthy, loving, prosperous, strong, creative and successful.

At school nobody taught us to plan our lives. No one suggested we should write down our own future goals. Once we have written something down the subconscious mind usually works out ways to get things done. Dream great dreams and write them down. As Picasso said: **"The first step is to have the dream."**

Most people take more time planning their vacation than they do planning their lives. Once you have experienced the benefits of goal setting you will do it on a regular basis. It shows you a method of developing options and choices rather than accepting a script for life that has been preplanned for you. We all evolve as a result of our childhood experiences, our education or economic circumstances and the influences of where and when we live. We might not be aware of other options. We accept much our parents and teachers tell us without question. We might be conditioned to want money, love, health, success and happiness but no one tells us how to plan our lives so we can obtain them.

Goal setting enables you to have priorities and to avoid spending time doing things that are irrelevant.

WHY SET GOALS?

You can either lead your life like a jelly fish in the ocean buffeted by the tides and waves or you can take control. You can learn to swim. Choose where you go and how you go. I was brought up with a fatalistic philosophy. It was as if I had no power to influence life's events. Some people are lucky some aren't. When I was 24, with a six-week-old baby daughter and an 18-month-old toddler my husband decided to fulfil his goal of studying for his medical degree. For the first time I understood the process of making a choice. We chose that he would stop work and start studying. We chose to take a risk. I undertook to fill the bread bin because I felt a sense of purpose in having a definitive goal. Once I accepted the responsibility of being the bread winner, I had to look for resourceful ways to earn a living. **There were no direct selling companies available where I lived in those days.**

After I started my own toy and craft business I began to develop my own practice of goal setting. I had something real to measure. **I set targets for my turnover.** I began to understand the power of holding an idea in my mind and acting to make it happen.

Many of us take on the process of goal setting in the material acquisition of a house, car or holiday. We now need to elevate this process to the more intangible areas of our lives. We can set a path of personal growth, business growth and relationship growth. There are also skills we can use to make goal setting far more effective and useful if we want to be the architects of our own destinies.

CREATE YOUR OWN ACTION CHART

- Decide what goals you want to achieve during a calendar year.
- Break up the goals into four, three-month sections. I find three months is a manageable time frame. It flows with the seasons and is not too long to work with.
- Divide the three months into three, one-month sections.
- Divide each month into four weeks.
- Decide what you need to do each week to reach your monthly goal.
- Review your pace and success in completing tasks as you go.

GOAL SETTING TECHNIQUES

CHOOSING GOALS

Most people think goals are an end in themselves that can be reached once and for all. In fact goals are more like road maps for progressing through life. **Each goal takes you part of the way by keeping you on course and making it harder to get lost.** Workable goals must be **measurable**; they must be concrete (write them down) and shared. A goal must also be **challenging**. We want to grow, extend ourselves and become enriched through accomplishing our goals.

MEASURABLE GOALS

Be sure to keep track of your progress. Break your project down into measurable units and keep evaluating how you are doing. Have one major goal and a few minor goals. Set a time frame for each one.

CONCRETE GOALS

Write down your goals as if they had been accomplished. **Begin with a vision of the end.** Imagine the reality of your goal. This makes them clear, precise and concrete. For example, I am an author, I am a speaker, I am a successful business person. By recording your goals you set in motion the process of becoming the person you want to be.

SHARE YOUR GOALS

"Tell somebody what you are going to do." This was one of Mary Kay's early lessons. **Broadcast your goals.** Don't keep them a secret. The expectations others have of your goals help you believe in doing them. The day I packed up my office three years ago, I was interviewed by a journalist. He asked me what I was going to do with my life as I had just sold my business. I told him I intended to write a book but I didn't want him to mention it in his article. He ignored me and wrote about the book in his published article. I began to get calls from friends asking me when my book would be completed. At that stage "the book" was a half-completed manuscript. I felt committed to perform and achieve my goal. I now had an audience with expectations. I had to complete the project.

USE YOUR STRENGTHS

Create your goals around your natural talents. Do what excites you. Do what gets the adrenalin going. Do what you feel good about. Stretch yourself but **capitalise on your strengths.** I have no musical ability. There would be no point in my trying to be a musician.

BE REALISTIC

Goals should be challenging but they should also be attainable. If you set unrealistic goals you sabotage yourself and become unhappy when things are not working out. Goals don't have to be easy. They can involve time, effort and energy but make sure they are real and valid.

LOGICAL STEPS

"Every journey begins with one small step."
Map out logical steps to help achieve your goal. Take action that will get you what you want. Be pro-active, make things happen. Take initiative.

Create momentum. Live, dream and believe in your goals every single day. Don't spend too much time on low priority items. Focus on the important tasks that will help take you closer to your goal. Decide what is the fastest and most efficient way to achieve your goal. Make sure you do not have to sacrifice the most valuable things in your life to achieve your goal. You might decide to take longer to achieve a goal so you still have time for your family.

Make sure you **enjoy the process of getting there**. The journey is as important as the destination. Make sure you know the difference between a goal and a fantasy. A fantasy is an idea you enjoy for sheer fun. A goal is a concrete, manageable concept.

COVER ALL AREAS OF YOUR LIFE

Intellectual goals	– Keep learning, studying and developing your mind.
Health goals	– Fitness, food, exercise, sleep, play, relaxation.
Relationship goals	– Improve and grow in an intimate relationship.
Social goals	– Meet people, keep in touch with friends, entertain.
Emotional goals	– Accept and express your feelings. – Develop courage. – Accept change and move on.
Career goals	– Develop your business and other contacts. – Increase your sales. – Develop skills, experience. – Become more effective in your work. – Strive for excellence.
Family goals	– Increase quality time spent with partner, children, parents and family.
Spiritual goals	– Get in touch with your inner being through meditation or religious involvement.
Financial goals	– Earn as much as you can. – Pay yourself first. – Save as much as you can. – Invest as much as you can. – Give as much as you can to charity.

- Write down all your dreams, visions, ideas and inspirations.
- Keep a pen and paper next to your bed.
- Review your goals regularly.
- Adapt, change and update your goals.
- List goals in the order you want to accomplish them.
- Break down each major goal into a time frame. Set a date by which you want it done.
- Create an action plan. Break down into small steps.
- Give yourself ten minutes per day when you can focus quietly on your goals. Add more, revamp and adapt.
- Keep a goal journal. You will become the author of your own life. Great goals attract energy of others who will help you. Clarity creates power. **If you expect a little you get a little. If you expect a lot you get a lot.**

CREATIVE VISUALISATION

Give yourself time to dream. You need to meditate, imagine, fantasise and visualise what you want. Great goals will provide an opportunity for personal growth. Draw a picture of your goal. Start with the end in mind. Visualise how you want things to be. Imagine all the details. Imagination can translate into reality.

Everything that happens in life starts as an IDEA in someone's head. You can choose which ideas become real. You control your pictures. Put your future in good hands, your own.

Shakti Gawain, in her classic book, **Creative Visualisation** shows us how to use our mental energy to transform ideas into reality. There is nothing magic or mystical in the process. It is a practical process we can all use. We already use our imagination every day.

I am now encouraging you to use visualisation as a conscious technique to create what you truly want: love, fulfilling work, health, prosperity, peace and harmony. Create an idea in your mind. Continue to focus on the picture regularly until it becomes a reality. Use your senses to see the picture and to imagine the feel, sound and smell of success.

ENERGY IS MAGNETIC

Thoughts and feelings have their own magnetic energy that attract energy of a similar nature. We can see this principle at work when we accidentally run into someone we've just been thinking of or happen to pick up a book that contains exactly the information we need at that moment. I have discovered that the more excited I am about an idea, the more coincidences and connections start to occur. The process of synchronicity takes place. The reason for this is that the thoughts become more powerful. The idea is a blue print. The architect starts with a plan. An artist starts with a vision.

As a result of **the law of attraction, we attract into our lives whatever we think about most on the deepest levels.** When we are negative, fearful and insecure we tend to attract the very experiences we are seeking to avoid. When we are positive in our attitude we attract people, situations and events that conform to our positive expectations.

USING CREATIVE VISUALISATION

* Find a comfortable position either sitting or lying in a quiet place where you won't be disturbed.
* Relax your body completely, letting all the tension flow out. Breathe deeply.
* Start to imagine the thing you want exactly as you would like it. Vividly create a picture in your mind.
* Have fun with it. Keep the image in your mind and make some positive, affirmative statements to yourself aloud.
* Don't resist doubts. Let them pass and go back to the most positive images.
* Do this for five minutes each day.

THE POWER OF INTENT

"Momentum – once you are moving in the direction of your goals nothing can stop you."

Often our well planned, brilliantly conceived and structured goals are discarded, diluted or just fade away before they reach maturity. WHY? The **power of intent** is lacking. In the absence of intent goals do not become reality. Intent transforms a possible idea to certainty. When we approach our goals with real intent in our thoughts, actions and words we release great power. It becomes impossible for us to be stopped. Another word for intent is willpower.

When we have intent we have every cell in our bodies at our command ready to accomplish our objectives. It is the power of intent that enables humans to perform super-human feats. Olympic athletes and all great achievers know how to harness this energy.

HOW TO GET INTENT

- You need clarity of purpose.
- Know what you want.
- Define your goal clearly, precisely.
- Be able to see the end in mind.
- Put all your energy on your goal.
- Concentrate on your goal.
- Cut out all conflicting or competing thoughts.
- Intent is more than just writing down goals. It is the process of using your will to make things happen.

COMMITMENT

Providence moves in at the moment we commit ourselves to a project with intent. All sorts of things happen to help us that would otherwise never have occurred. All manner of unforeseen incidents, meetings and assistance come our way. We label these events, coincidences.

A simple example of creative visualisation and the power of intent was brought to me recently. When I separated from my husband I moved into a rented apartment. I wanted to buy a home but I did not know where I wanted to live, how much I wanted to spend or whether I wanted a house, town house or unit. I also did not know when I wanted to move.

For five months I went hunting every Saturday. My energies were splintered. I looked without success. In November I had a speaking engagement in Tasmania. I was driving along the beautiful Tasmanian countryside between Launceston and Hobart. My mind was drifting. I began to focus on the prospect of moving and finding a home. I formed a clear vision of the street I wanted to live in, the amount I wanted to spend and the type of apartment I wanted to buy.

A day later I drove from the airport, went straight to a real estate office and told the estate agent what I wanted. He knew of just the place for me. Within five minutes of seeing it I knew it was mine. There was no doubt. The price was right. The time of the year was perfect. Everything worked smoothly.

This would not have happened if I had not had total **CLARITY OF VISION**, a clear picture of what I wanted. I have now lived in this apartment for several months and I am incredibly happy and comfortable.

WRITE YOUR OWN SCRIPT

Whichever way we look at our lives, we don't have to be the continuous victims of fate or luck. We can script our own lives in the way an actor brings a play to life. All we need is the imagination to project ourselves into the scenario. Write down a detailed picture of how you would like your life to be and an action plan to get you there.

AFFIRMATIONS

Keep repeating positive words, phrases and images to yourself. I learnt the power of affirmations when I started jogging. As I ran I would tell myself: "Keep going Cyndi, I know you can. Don't stop, keep going. Fly faster." Before I knew it I had reached my destination. **Positive self talk is very reinforcing.** This is the message your subconscious responds to. Affirm yourself with every thought.

CHAPTER 6

THE CHALLENGE OF CHANGE

CHALLENGE OF CHANGE

Change is inevitable. No one is a stranger to change. There is no way we can halt the process of change. How can we learn to participate actively in the process of change instead of resisting it?

In this chapter I will outline some of the keys to facing change in a positive way. We can learn to embrace change and enjoy the excitement and challenge of letting go and moving on to bigger and better experiences.

We all love the comfort of familiar places, faces and activities. We all feel anxiety at the prospect of moving house, moving suburb, city, country, job or career. Yet, when I consider my own life all my greatest opportunities and most rewarding experiences have come about through dramatic change. We can make it easier for ourselves to embrace change, create change and in so doing enjoy a life that is full of choices and fresh options.

Something in your life may need changing. It might be a relationship, a job or even your own attitude. Change is not easy. There are many obstacles to overcome. Now is the perfect time to start. We all feel degrees of insecurity about new situations. The only way to overcome the fear is to act as soon as possible.

Changing to a career in direct selling from whatever profession or job you currently hold will require the courage to take a risk. You are challenging your own abilities and performance. This requires that you have to believe in yourself and be motivated to make a commitment to your new career.

HANDLING FEAR

If you knew you could handle anything that came your way, what would you have to fear? The answer is nothing. Fear is only a state of mind. We need to develop more trust in our ability to handle whatever comes our way.

Mothers instil fear into us. Fear of getting lost, fear of not handling situations, fear of risks. We need to unlearn this behaviour. I had an over protective mother. "Be careful. I'm so worried," she'd say. I worried so much about her being worried that I could not have fun. It took me many years of independence to realise whatever happens to me, I can handle it. I keep saying to myself, "I'll handle it".

As I began to do things on my own I began to taste the deliciousness of emerging self-confidence. It is not all comfortable. It is like learning to ride a bicycle or to ski. You fall frequently, pick yourself up and try again. With each little step you will feel more confident. We can't escape fear but we can transform it into a companion that accompanies us in all our exciting adventures. The more you confront fear, the more likely you are to succeed and the more confidence you have to try new directions. Whenever I feel my fear returning, I think back to some of the changes I made and how they always worked out in a positive way.

* I emigrated from South Africa to Australia.
* I changed careers from teaching to starting a business.
* From the toy industry to being an author.
* From being an author to being a speaker.
* From living in one suburb for nine years to a new area.
* From being married to being single.
* From being single to a relationship of intimacy.

All these new directions had a phase of decision making. There was always a set of unknowns to address: insecurities, risks and fears to conquer.

I have learnt

* To say yes to many new challenges.
* To take more control over my life.
* To make my dreams a reality.
* To become more assertive.

Do you want to connect with the **"powerhouse"** within, raise your self-esteem and experience more enjoyment? To do this you have to allow yourself to let go, take risks and step out of your comfort zone.

Susan Jeffers has written an inspiring book called **Feel the Fear and Do It Anyway**. It is a guide to turning your fear and indecision into confidence and action. Her techniques show us how to turn that feeling of paralysis into action. We need some tools to assist us in the process of change. The first and most important component is to develop the quality of courage.

As I spoke to audiences across the country about the experience of **Feel the Fear and Do It Anyway**, I sensed women reaching out to me. We were all struggling with the same conflicts. We were all consumed by fear of change when we confronted a new experience. We need to develop techniques for taking control of our lives by handling the process of change.

HOW TO BE COURAGEOUS

Courage is not a feeling. **It is an act of doing what you feel is right despite your fears.** The greater the fear the greater the courage necessary to overcome it and to do the right thing. Most great heroes will reveal how frightened they are at the time of performing their most heroic acts. Bravery is the action they take despite the fear. Kay Cottee who sailed single handed around the world in a yacht tells how terrified she was alone, struck by storms with the elements battering her boat. Gaby Kennard, who flew alone around the world describes her fear at certain dangerous points in her journey. All great and courageous acts require that you feel the fear and do it anyway!

FEAR IS HERE TO STAY

Fear will never go away as long as we are growing and changing. As long as we undertake new challenges we will experience the emotion of fear. As a professional speaker, I still experience the same fear before I speak in front of a new audience. The fear is partly anticipation, partly the desire to perform and do my best. The only way to eliminate the fear is to go out and do it. What we need to do is reverse our behaviour. Instead of moving away from fear we should move towards it. Fear embraces our new challenges and with that our new goals. We can confront fear from a position of choice or stay immobile and helpless. Being stuck causes us to feel depressed, hopeless and ineffective. As Susan Jeffers says: **"The secret is to move fear from a position of pain to a position of power".**

WOMEN AND POWER

Women have been conditioned to think power is unfeminine and unattractive. Quite the reverse is true. A woman who is assertive, who has choices and is in control of her life, draws others like a magnets. People love positive energy. A woman who is decisive radiates confidence and exudes a magic quality that captivates and encourages others to want to be part of her orbit.

"Angels fly because they take themselves lightly." When I heard this it stuck a chord in my soul. We all carry around too much baggage from the past. We need to know what to let go. We need to let go relationships that don't work for us, clothes that no longer suit us, habits that are ineffective. We need to play with life instead of fighting it.

We all have this little voice inside us saying, "Don't move, don't change, don't take risks. You might make a mistake." **The biggest mistake you can make is not to try.**

"It is not because things are difficult that we do not dare. It is because we do not dare that they are difficult." We need to change our thoughts so we are thinking: "I can, I know I'll handle it because I'm responsible for my own life."

HOW TO BEGIN TO CHANGE

"Today is the first day of the rest of your life."

- Believe in yourself and your ability to change.
- Take responsibility for your own life.
- Don't blame others or play martyr.
- Decide what you want.
- Change your thoughts
- Change your responses.
- Don't procrastinate with decision making.
- Let go of people, places, clothes and habits which no longer serve you in a constructive way.
- Ask for support and encouragement.

KEYS TO THE PROCESS OF CHANGE

- Set realistic goals.
- Start small.
- Be patient.
- Be persistent.
- Don't compare yourself with others.
- Keep a journal of your progress.
- Go to a support group where you can share experiences.
- Be kind to yourself.
- Reward yourself en route.
- **Start now – there is no more perfect time to begin.**

TOOLS TO ASSIST US IN THE PROCESS OF CHANGE

- Motivational tapes.
- Positive quotes.
- Inspirational books and biographies of other achievers.
- Encouraging friends.
- Mentors and role models.
- Positive affirmations.
- Music.
- Meditation.
- Exercise.

WIDEN YOUR COMFORT ZONE

Do something each day which makes you feel uncomfortable. We all have more power than we could ever have imagined to change aspects of our lives.

TAKE A RISK A DAY

* Speak to a stranger in the supermarket, an elevator or in the train.
* Buy a new brand of product.
* Buy a shirt in a colour you have never worn.
* Read a new author.
* Eat something different, new or unusual.
* Exercise a bit longer.
* Wear your hair differently.
* Change the colour of your lipstick, eye shadow or nail polish.

MAKING A DECISION

* Explore the alternatives.
* Talk to people, get other opinions.
* Establish priorities.
* Write down your options in two columns. Write the pros on one side and the cons on the other. You will be amazed how easily the answers to your decisions will emerge.
* Look for feedback from other sources.
* Meditate or pray (as appropriate).

CREATE YOUR OWN CHANGE

We can't change the world but we can change ourselves. At 20 I was a great idealist. I believed I could change the world. At 40 I'm a great realist because **the only person I know I can change is myself.**

We need to break old habits and try some new behaviours. We can create new responses. It is easier and more comfortable to keep doing familiar things.

The road to fulfilment is within your reach. Once you become aware you have choices and options you can start to move. Many people who are stuck are only in a dead end situation because they won't allow themselves to take advantage of new opportunities.

The purpose of this chapter has been to help you handle change in a way that enables you to move forward. Each time you have the courage to take on a new challenge your self esteem is raised considerably. You will survive no matter what happens. **Security is not in having things, its in handling situations.**

CHAPTER 7

CREATING CHARISMA

LOOKING GOOD, FEELING GREAT

"What you are shouts so loudly I cannot hear what you say." Ralph Waldo Emerson.

When a woman feels she looks good she radiates self confidence. She walks with her head held high and she feels happy with her image in the mirror. I love charismatic, attractive people. I love people whose presence lights up the room. Some people radiate an aura which makes us want to be around them. What are these magic, indefinable aspects of a personality which draw us to people?

It isn't only physical beauty which appeals to us. People who are confident and believe in themselves express this special quality. We enjoy being with people who believe in their own abilities because it makes us feel secure. **We become inspired and energised by charismatic people and they motivate us to emulate them.**

We are not discussing the superficial aspects of a person's looks. We are looking at a person as a whole package. Your image is made up of:

* How you look.
* What you are wearing.
* Body language.
* The personality you project.

"Meeting him was like opening a bottle of champagne." Winston Churchill on meeting Franklin D Roosevelt.

FIRST IMPRESSIONS

You never have a second chance to make a first impression.

There is no doubt first impressions are very important. The image you project through your visible appearance is the first message you send in any new situation. Looking the part is as important as being the part. You can cultivate attractiveness based on good grooming, clever selection of clothes, taking care of your body and developing a sense of individual style.

ALWAYS LOOK YOUR BEST

My Brazilian grandmother, Rosa was 90 last birthday. She gets up each day, bathes, does her hair, dresses and puts on makeup. She then cleans her house and does her own cooking. No matter what time of the day you call on her, you will not catch her off guard. She always looks her best. She looks 30 years younger than she is. She does not think of herself as old and she maintains good health.

While appearance is not everything, a first impression is very powerful. When people look good they feel good. They feel more positive about themselves and they often achieve better results.

In the direct selling business, there are many days when you are working at home alone. There does not seem any reason to be dressed up but I believe you should exercise the discipline of getting dressed; made up and looking good every single day. Even if you spend the day making phone calls, make an effort to look good so **you can project a confident professional image**.

TRENDY BASICS

Today's trend is to wear work clothes in the evening and on weekends. The idea behind this is to have a number of good quality basic pieces that can be combined to produce a variety of different looks, both casual and smart.

10 MAGIC PIECES

1. Basic navy blazer (well cut wool).
2. White T-shirt.
3. White classic shirt.
4. Black or navy polo neck.
5. Black tailored trousers.
6. Straight black skirt.
7. Classic black or navy evening dress.
8. Black or navy pleated skirt.
9. Denim jeans.
10. Silk evening shirt in favourite colour.

With different scarves, belts and accessories, this type of wardrobe can take you through a variety of seasons, occasions and times of day.

BUILDING A WARDROBE

Try not to shop on impulse or haphazardly. It will turn out to be an expensive exercise. Sale bargains are not always as cheap as they seem if you never wear them. Here is a great tip I was given: **Don't buy something unless it goes with three other garments in your wardrobe.** Think about your clothes as a long term investment. Collect classics, buy quality and build on a base. One season you might buy three items, next season you add to the base.

FASHION AWARENESS

Fashion awareness indicates an understanding of contemporary trends, new looks and an openness to adapt your style. You need to be ready to change your image. People become tired of always seeing you look the same. Look at fashion magazines to get ideas.

WAYS TO CHANGE YOUR LOOK

* Change your hair style.
* Change your hair colour.
* Change the colour of your make up.
* Change your skirt length.
* Change the shape of your jacket.
* Use different accessories with your clothes.
* Wear an unusual colour.
* Create changes with belts, scarves, fun stockings, costume jewellery, hats and sunglasses.

CREATING STYLE

Style is more than the clothes we wear. Style is an understanding of how to incorporate a certain fashion look. It is the knowledge of knowing your best features, of highlighting your assets. It is a feel for the elements which go together to create your image. If you don't know what colours or styles suit you, go to a fashion consultant and get help.

I love dramatic clothes. I have a very clear picture of the styles that suit my personality. I love flamboyant earrings, bright colours and well fitted jackets with short skirts. I wear exotic jewel colours such as emerald, magenta, purple, turquoise and bright tangerine. I enjoy all-in-one jump suits in soft fabrics because I love ease of movement and the fact that with one garment I am dressed.

Find your style. Feeling and looking good on the outside goes a long way towards building inner confidence and self assurance.

YOUR HOME ENVIRONMENT

Style is not only limited to what you wear but also how you live. Your environment includes not only your mental and emotional environment but also your physical living space. You need to create a sense of harmony and peace in your life.

Beautiful objects, things we love and soft welcoming colours create an ambience in which we can flourish. Make sure your environment is a reflection of your personality.

PUT ON A HAPPY FACE

A simple smile is the most powerful tool you have. Don't forget to use it. It is amazing but the process of smiling makes you feel good. People respond positively to a smile. **It lights up your face and their lives.** Even if someone doesn't smile back you have not lost anything. Anita Roddick, founder of the Body Shop instructs all her employees to smile as part of their customer service.

PERSONALITY

Dare to be different. Express your uniqueness, don't be afraid to project and express your personality. One speaker I know always wears gorgeous hats.

EXERCISE, FITNESS AND HEALTH

I am an exercise fanatic! I became addicted to exercise after being a very unsporty person. I have bad co-ordination and struggle to hit a tennis ball, golf ball or do any sport which requires great skill. A neighbour introduced me to jogging. At the time I had a two-year-old and a baby. The escape inherent in spending 20 minutes on my own running away from my full time responsibilities was very attractive in itself. The other rewards, fitness, health and more energy came later. By then I was a dedicated jogger. If you want to run a business and expose yourself to a demanding life style, you need energy. **Exercise provides this energy**, increases endurance and strengthens your body and spirit. When you have your health your potential is unlimited.

GUIDELINES FOR EXERCISING

- Have a health check with your doctor.
- Choose an activity you enjoy.
- Choose a time of day you can adhere to.
- Start by doing a little and gradually increase.

- Set yourself attainable short-term goals.
- Occasionally exercise with a friend in pleasant surroundings.
- Music is a great asset to exercise. I run with earphones and find the music a great companion.
- Explore a few different types of exercise and find out what suits your temperament or schedule.

LOOKING AFTER YOUR BODY

Taking care of your body is one of the most fundamental ways in which you can convince yourself of your value as a person. The health of the mind and body are inextricably linked. When we experience stress or emotional problems it usually expresses itself in the form of an illness or disease. Not caring about your body is usually a reflection of low self esteem. It is also a vicious circle. If we don't keep our bodies healthy and in shape, we feel negative and unhappy about ourselves.

Adequate exercise improves your heart and lung capacity, increases your resistance to disease and regulates your metabolism. It also gives you more energy to achieve your goals.

There are many choices available depending on your needs, time availability, preferences and life style.

Here are some of your options.

*	aerobics	*	power walking	*	yoga
*	dancing	*	swimming	*	gymnastics
*	cycling	*	karate	*	netball
*	squash	*	tennis	*	aquarobics
*	belly dancing				

TIME FOR EXERCISE IS ALSO TIME OUT FOR YOURSELF.

It reduces stress and allows you to have fun and relax. You can either incorporate exercise into a social activity or use it as time to meditate and be alone.

ALLOWING YOURSELF TO BE LOOKED AFTER

We all need love, care, support and nurturing. As women, we are conditioned to give love and support to those around us. We need to learn how to receive this kind of nurturing as we might not get all the support we need from one source. It is important to know how to get our needs met.

Getting comfort from people who care takes us a long way to feeling better. We need to learn to ask for help.

WHERE CAN WE DRAW SUPPORT?

- friends
- parents
- children
- partners
- ourselves
- spiritual activities

- hairdressers
- masseurs
- work colleagues
- magazines, books and tapes
- groups we attend

THE WHOLE PACKAGE

Your self-image determines how you see yourself. It is a creation you have developed over the years. It is the response to events and experiences that have imprinted themselves on you. You can expand your self-image. You can create a new self-image by changing the thoughts you have about yourself. I realise that at age 40 I am attracting different responses from others than I did at 20. What seems to draw people to me are my inner qualities. I am now internally richer and more confident.

Realise that people respond to the whole package. They are attracted to the way you look, the way you move, the smile, the voice and the energy which you radiate. If you are tight, closed and introverted, they cannot reach you. Aim to become someone about whom others say: "She's one of those women who walks into a room and the air shimmers" or "She has this presence". See yourself as a whole. We tend to analyse or get "hung up" about one aspect of ourselves. Learn to project your inner being through your body language, your voice and let your individuality shine through.

COMMUNICATION SKILLS

Public speaking is the second biggest fear in the world next to death. Conquer it. Don't worry about mistakes. The audience don't know what you mean to say.

Public speaking skills are essential for business building. If you plan, prepare and rehearse you can conquer the butterflies. If you genuinely love your audience, want to help them and feel passionately about your subject, your fear will vanish.

Visibility is necessary for success. Develop a clear and eloquent speaking style. Dress in a way that reflects the image you want to project especially when you are up on the stage. It is important to look good.

PREPARE THOROUGHLY

When preparing a presentation for a group prepare thoroughly:
1. Jot down all the points you need to cover.
2. Analyse the purpose of your talk, make it clear.
3. Create an introduction, three main points and a conclusion.
4. Don't try and say too much.
5. Always have something left to say at the end.
6. If you have facts, figures, recognitions and sales it is perfectly appropriate to read them.
7. Prepare your points on cards.
8. Use personal stories, anecdotes or incidents to illustrate a point.
9. Pause with a short silence rather than "um ah".
10. Repeat your main points, sum up and end on a high note.

SPEAK FROM THE HEART

All speakers experience stage fright but we learn how to handle it. Dottie Walters, who is a world expert on teaching presentation skills says: "Professional speaking is a daring business, so stage fright or no stage fright, you must be willing to stand up **and speak from your heart** to the audience".

USING AN EXCITING VOCABULARY

As a speaker, words are the tools of my trade. I am always looking for new, interesting and vivid words. I keep a log book of positive words that I can keep adding to my motivational presentations. Become a collector of words. Use words from different sources and keep a thesaurus nearby. This will give you alternative words for the words you may already have used in your presentation. Always look for new and different ways of saying things. Introduce the drama of theatre into your presentation. **Dramatise, emphasise and project your personality.**

TECHNIQUES FOR VOICE PROJECTION

* Learn to use your voice with expression.
* Don't speak in a monotone.
* Vary the tone.
* Vary the pace.
* Speak in an even pitch.
* Speak clearly, open your mouth.

GOLDEN RULES FOR MAKING A PRESENTATION

1. Take a few deep breaths before you start.
2. Close your eyes for one minute before you go up.
3. Focus on your first few words only.
4. Once you have mastered these confidently, you are on your way and the rest will flow.
5. In your mind realise that even though there is a whole audience in front of you, you are speaking to each person one on one. This is less daunting.
6. Smile, let the audience feel your presence, enjoy yourself.
7. Watch your body language, stand composed.
8. Join a group like Toastmasters for practice in speaking to a group.
9. Make eye contact with a few faces in the audience.
10. Practise and rehearse your initial presentations until you feel comfortable with an audience. Enjoy yourself and relax. Speak at a comfortable pace, don't rush your presentation.

THE ART OF SELLING TO A WOMAN

CHAPTER 8

SELLING STRATEGIES

NOTHING HAPPENS WITHOUT A SALE

Selling is the very **"HEART OF BUSINESS"**. But most women's first reaction is, "I couldn't possibly sell". This response is most common among women who have never been in business. Very few women have been conditioned to think selling is a worthwhile profession. Few of us fantasised about a career in sales. We thought about glamour industries. We did not know the glamour, opportunity and possibilities inherent in a selling career.

In today's market everyone has to sell themselves first. Whether you are a doctor, a lawyer, an accountant or a professional in another field, you have to go out and market your services. The reputation of the selling industry has been less than rosy. Throughout history there have been unscrupulous sales people and in the past sales training has been basic and limited. "Close the sale" was the basis of most techniques. People believe it implies pressure. **"Nobody wants to be sold but everybody loves to buy,"** says the author Helen Bruveris. **We need to create an environment where the customer wants to buy.**

A happy customer will return. She will share the joy of her purchase with friends. In this chapter you will learn how to develop a winning sales personality and how to create the right attitude towards your product and your customer.

Selling is the essential business skill. Selling is the combination of you, your attitude, your goals, your product knowledge, your people skills and the ability to manage a sales team. **Selling today is the art of developing relationships with customers.**

YOUR ATTITUDE DETERMINES YOUR ALTITUDE

YOUR APPEARANCE

Attractiveness can be acquired. Whatever product you are selling you are also **selling yourself**. A well presented exterior takes you a long way. You need to look well groomed, smart and stylish. As we said in the chapter on image, **"You never get a second chance to make a first impression"**. Coco Chanel said: "If a woman looks cheap they notice her clothes, if she looks good, they notice the woman". Women can look feminine without looking provocative. In selling to other women you want to look good without looking over dressed. The way you look impacts on how other women feel about themselves. When I see an elegant well-groomed woman with a stylish image I become inspired to improve my own look. If you dress as if you are successful you will inspire confidence in other women. Make the most of yourself, go regularly for hair styling, facials and keep your wardrobe ready for action.

YOUR VOICE

The way you use your voice when making a sales presentation goes a long way towards ensuring someone will enjoy listening to you.

* Don't talk in a monotone.
* Vary your pitch.
* Don't use a high pitched shrill.
* Keep your voice even, soothing and well modulated.
* Don't talk too fast.
* **Listening is more important than talking.**

MENTAL ATTITUDE

1. Analyse yourself.
2. Know unshakingly what you want.
3. **Write down** your goals and action plans.
4. Draw up an action plan for your sales goals.
5. Break the plan up into **manageable steps**.
6. Start from where you are now.
7. Review your plans often.
8. Make sure you are **enthusiastic** about people.
9. Choose products you can **use and love**.
10. **Go the extra mile** for your customer.

INTEGRITY

Be yourself. Let your own friendly personality shine through and maintain a sense of honesty and openness. One of my friends says I can sell ice cubes to Eskimos. That is only because I sell myself each time.

You need to stand by your word, keep promises and maintain your integrity. Don't make false claims about your product or services. Don't promise deliveries you can't meet and don't go back on your word.

OPENNESS TO OPPORTUNITIES

When you are selling a product you are always prospecting and looking for new customers. You are always on the alert. When meeting people socially, ask questions and find out what they do and who they know. Build up a bank of contacts. Read, travel, visit new places and keep abreast of all commercial developments so new opportunities are always on the horizon. Be aware. Read local papers, listen for trends. Keep in touch with the pulse of what is happening.

HUMOUR

I believe humour is not only the key to selling, but also the secret of all effective inter-personal skills. My father had a wonderful sense of humour and he taught me to laugh at myself and with others in situations that could be considered bleak.

Business involves relating to people. Get someone to laugh. Take away the seriousness of it all. Put them at ease. Relax them. If you have a low-key repertoire of jokes, use them if you feel you need to take the tension away or break the ice.

BELIEVE IN YOURSELF

You need to have inner strength and be confident of your own ability when you sell. You will have to cope with rejection as a continual part of your role. You need to maintain your positive self-esteem and not give in to negative responses.

EMOTIONAL ATTITUDE

To be an effective sales person you need a **positive** and **enthusiastic** attitude. Many of the attributes related to being a successful entrepreneur are found in a good sales person. You also need **stamina** and energy to keep going. If you call on ten customers you might get nine rejections and then one fantastic order. You need **staying power** to keep going when you get turned down. You eventually develop a thick hide. It would be emotionally tiring to be devastated by each rejection. If you believe in your product and yourself you will eventually succeed. **If you can't have a love affair with your product don't start selling.**

You need **courage**. You are exploring new territory and always investigating new avenues. You also need to be **self-disciplined** and to keep pursuing your goal in the face of failure. My motto has always been: **"Turn every 'No' into 'Yes'"**. Eventually someone is going to buy what you have to sell. If you give up you will never know what success may be waiting in store for you.

THE "P's" OF POSITIVE ATTITUDE

* Persistence	* Promise	* Proactive
* Perseverance	* People	* Profits
* Power	* Potential	* Possibilities
* Potency	* Product	* Personality
* Pizzazz	* Priorities	* Passion
* Panache	* Professional	* Presentation

THE ART OF SELLING TO A WOMAN

In her classic book, **Never Underestimate the Selling Power of a Woman, Dottie Walters** says: "In every sales situation there is a buyer and a seller. If you have trouble selling to a woman it simply means that she has turned the situation around and has sold you on her **'no'** answer."

Women today have control over the buying power of our country. As women with predominantly female customers you need to find ways to appeal to a woman's needs.

WHAT DO WOMEN REALLY BUY

Women do not buy a product or service. They buy the image of what they want to be. **A woman's life has a forward motion to it.** She wants to be slimmer, younger, more beautiful, a better wife, mother, lover and home maker. She wants more approval in the eyes of the people that matter. She wants more time. Most women would easily see the value of buying a microwave, washing machine, dishwasher and vacuum cleaner. They are all time saving devices that offer her a beautiful home with ease and in less time. Why would a woman buy cosmetics, make-up or perfume? Because they promise to make her more attractive, more desirable to men and look younger. Who doesn't want to feel good?

Talk to your customer. Try to find out how she sees herself or wants to see herself and sell her that vision. Make her feel special. **Customer service is about caring for her needs in a personal way.**

The simple process of complimenting a woman makes her feel special. Be genuine and sincere. There is nothing worse than an insincere salesperson.

WHY WOMEN BUY

What motivates people? What do women really want?
- They want love, romance and pleasure.
- They want time for themselves.
- They want to be beautiful, younger, more desirable.
- They want health, peace of mind, safety, security.
- They want to have fun, enjoyment, entertainment, the prospect of excitement
- They want something to look forward to
- They want achievement, recognition.

YOUR FEMALE PROSPECTS

She has a multitude of personalities. She is a little girl who needs to be admired and protected, she is a teenager full of giggles and flirtation, a mother who needs to comfort, nurture and inspire, a wife who stands by her man, an old lady who needs to be consulted and respected. At any moment you can see a combination of all facets of her personality.

KEYS TO A WOMAN'S HEART

Find out about your potential customer or prospect. Is she a homemaker, married or single, working in a career or profession, adolescent or mature? When you sell to a man you sell him on the practical features and benefits of a product. When you sell to a woman you sell something more intangible. A woman buys beauty, atmosphere and a promise.
- Put a woman at her ease.
- Agree early on in the conversation. Listen, let her talk and ask as many open-ended questions as you can in a low key manner.
- Ask a woman to help you. Make her feel needed.
- Women have a basic curiosity. Arouse her curiosity.
- Make a friend of your customer.
- Act with compassion and caring.
- Service your customer. You are there to help.
- Vary your approach to suit the woman's age group.
- Treat her as an individual.

PRODUCT KNOWLEDGE

Retailing product to customers is the basis of your business.

- If you don't use your products you have little chance of succeeding in this business. Use your products.
- Develop as much product knowledge as you can.
- Know the benefits of the products.
- Carry brochures, leaflets and samples with you.
- Keep abreast of product launches.
- Get to know your company's promotions and special offers.
- Be enthusiastic about your products.
- Love your products. They are the driving force of your business.

CUSTOMER SERVICE

Think about why a customer would prefer to purchase her cosmetics or jewellery from you rather than go to a retail store: convenience, value and quality. But the big drawcard is **personal service**. Think about how you can effectively service your customers, build loyalty and create a situation where you can anticipate their needs. Most women today are concerned about saving time. Shopping retail involves much wasted time and often little service. Capitalise on these two aspects of direct selling. **Give prompt, efficient service and turn your customer into a friend.**

SELLING SKILLS

The selling process has three main phases, the opening, the benefits and the close.

THE OPENING

During the opening phase ask as many questions as possible to establish the customer's needs. This gives you the information you require to make a successful sale. Ask the customer about her habits, health, lifestyle, work and family. Relate the questions to the product you are selling. For example, if you are selling cosmetics, ask the customer about her skin type or sensitivity. What make-up is she currently using? This leads to the next phase in the selling process.

THE BENEFITS

Translate the features of your product to your customer in terms of benefits by knowing their needs. For example, if you are selling vitamins the benefit to your customer is good health. If you are selling skincare products, the benefit is a beautiful glowing skin. With car care products, the benefits are increased economy, better fuel consumption, less frequent servicing and a longer lifespan for the vehicle.

THE CLOSE

Recognise buying signals. This is the time to close the sale. **Remember a number of small "yeses" add up to one big "yes".** When your customer expresses specific interest in features of the product, reinforce this interest and close the sale. For example, "In which shades of pink is this lipstick available?" Answer the question simply and ask the customer how many she would like.

Any objections at this point should be handled without coming into conflict with the customer. Objections are often the customer's desire for more information or reassurance. **Don't take objections as a personal attack or rejection.**

The purpose of closing the sale is to **help the customer make a decision** as easily and quickly as possible. While the customer is undecided, she is out of balance and in a state of stress. By helping her come to a final decision, you are restoring her balance.

OVERCOMING SALES RESISTANCE

1. Find out why you got a no. Some people automatically say "no" to everyone. **"No" does not always mean "no".** Know when to leave your customer alone and when to persevere.
2. Talk to a woman about herself and she will listen for hours.
3. Capture her attention.
4. Fire her imagination.
5. Repeat the benefits of the product. Tell her how excited you are about your company and products.
6. Build trust.
7. Talk your customer's language. Pick up on their words and repeat them.
8. Believe in your product and yourself and be genuinely friendly and sincere.
9. You are there to solve her problem. Tailor your pitch to suit her needs.
10. Keep asking questions to which she will have to answer **"yes"**. It will create a **"yes"** attitude.

MAXIMISE YOUR TELEPHONE TIME

There is no tool as effective in selling as the correctly used telephone.

HOW TO GET MORE BUSINESS BY TELEPHONE

1. Smile when you talk to a customer on the telephone. Smiling when you talk will be reflected in your voice.
2. Give your customer your full attention.
3. Work out the points of the discussion before you make the call.
4. Make a list of all the customers you are going to call, the date and their phone numbers.
5. Have their customer cards out when you call.
6. Make notes as you speak.
7. Relax, be cheerful, pleasant and enthusiastic.
8. Vary the tone of your voice, keep your voice low.
9. Morning or in the early evening is the best time to call. Don't call after 9pm.
10. When you are soliciting on the phone for appointments, just sell the appointment. Don't try to make the entire sale. Be a good listener, be courteous.

KEEPING SALES RECORDS

Remember these three words **"WRITE IT DOWN"** at the moment it happens. We always think we will remember things but we rarely do. Get down everything in black and white so you can keep accurate records. Make a carbon copy of each sale in an invoice book. Find a system of customer records that works for you.

CUSTOMER FILES

Create customer prospect cards. On each card record your customer's name, address, telephone number, the amount of her last purchase, the date of purchase and products selected. **This enables you to carry out efficient customer service.**

Keep alphabetical customer files and an invoice book. Start from the first day. The greater your business becomes, the greater your need to keep accurate records. These records will also be useful for your accountant at the end of each financial year.

Good Records Allow You To:
* Service your customers efficiently.
* Organise your time and effort.
* Look at your work objectively.
* Analyse your sales and see which products are selling well.
* Keep track of your commissions.
* Think about a different approach next time.

At the beginning of each month, go through your contacts, your customer cards, your calender of commitments and work out where you need to spend your energy if you want to achieve your goals. Work out a schedule to allow you to cover effectively your territory, demonstrations, networking functions and telephone sales.

Create a monthly plan of work. At the end of each month, total your invoiced sales and evaluate it against the goals you set.

THE IMPORTANCE OF SALES MEETINGS

As a new consultant it is vital to **go to as many sales meetings as possible.** This enables you to build up your product knowledge, form a closer association with the company and meet other successful direct selling consultants and managers.

At meetings you will also get:
* Motivation to develop your business.
* Inspiration from other speakers and role models.
* A sense of momentum for your business.
* Reward and recognition for your achievement.
* News about company seminars.
* Special promotions.
* New product launches.
* A feeling of belonging to the company.

Take advantage of any regular sales training offered. Listen to tapes, read motivational books, go to workshops and seminars.

Participate as much as you can. Share your problems and **ask for help. This is your support group.** Your leader is there to help you.

CHAPTER 9

PUTTING ON THE SHOW

THE OPPORTUNITY SHOWCASE

An opportunity showcase is an evening where you invite newcomers and your team to hear about your business. **John Kalench** in his book, **Being the Best You can be in MLM**, says the following of an opportunity showcase: "This acts like a transformer that dramatically boosts the energy of success for everybody involved. Once a month everybody shows up looking great, sounding even better and sharing their success with everyone else."

The more people you can muster the better. This is an evening for team members, newcomers and potential prospects. Synergy creates and sustains momentum. This is the unique ability of a whole to be greater than the sum of the individual parts.

The futurist, Buckminster Fuller brought **the concept of synergy** into popular awareness. The more people present at an opportunity showcase, the more excitement, enthusiasm and commitment is generated. It is also an excellent venue to highlight the products of the company, the philosophy and share the successes of those already in the business. This can often be **much more powerful** to a potential new distributor than a one on one meeting. This adds an empowering dimension to your business when it matters most: at the beginning. Now people will be able to look around and see others who have built businesses. This will give new prospects confidence in the company.

THE ELEMENTS OF A GOOD SHOWCASE

A good showcase is a work of art but there are many basic ingredients every showcase should contain.

* Choose an up market venue, hotel or reception room.
* Make sure there is safe, easy parking close by.
* Create a reception area to greet each new arrival.
* Give each person a name tag, one colour for existing members and another for newcomers. This will enable newcomers to approach experienced people.
* Use lively music. It sets a great tone to the evening.
* Create a comprehensive, attractive product display. Use props and make sure the display is eye catching and visually dramatic.
* Put out less chairs rather than more. This makes the room look full and gives the expectation that more have turned up than were anticipated. Keep spare chairs stacked for extra guests.

* Start and end on time.
* Keep the formal part of the evening under an hour.
* Maintain the energy level.
* Serve refreshments such as tea, coffee and juice afterwards and encourage guests to stay, mingle and ask questions.

FORMAT

1. Introduce the evening and welcome everyone. Choose a first speaker who has considerable **warmth, energy and enthusiasm**. The speaker should cover basic elements of the business opportunity including the company philosophy, products and marketing plan. **DO NOT GO INTO ANY DETAIL ON ANY OF THESE AREAS.** Newcomers will not remember. Rather create curiosity, excitement and give a broad overview.

2. **Use stories and anecdotes** that are relevant wherever possible. Give them concrete information such as the size of the company, number of distributors, efficiency of the company. Paint a picture of security, stability and make them feel comfortable with the company.

3. Invite a number of successful distributors to come up for a minute each and tell their stories. Don't start with your high fliers. **Start with someone who has achieved small success** and build up to the mega-successes. This enables newcomers not to be intimidated. They can identify with small achievements first and they will say to themselves, "**I can do this.** This is not so difficult". **Use the inspirational sales leaders near the end.** This is a much more powerful technique. It also leaves new prospects with a feeling of excitement and heady with possibilities. **People love success stories.**

4. **ALLOW FOR QUESTIONS.** I have found a very useful exercise for questions is to create half a dozen of my own and hand them out before the start of the meeting. I number the questions and make sure the last question has answers which will leave the audience on an 'up'. This serves two functions. First it takes away the uncomfortable feelings in a group when no-one has the courage to ask the first question. Once the first few questions roll, the audience relaxes and starts generating their own questions. It also allows you to keep control of the proceedings until the end. Conclude with a thank you and details of the next opportunity showcase, any special training sessions and an invitation to talk in more depth at the back of the room later.

5. **Keep the energy up.** Close the meeting before they have had enough. Put on the music again and invite all guests to stay for refreshments.

TRADE SHOWS, BRIDAL FAIRS, EXHIBITIONS

With direct selling, your purpose is to expand your customer base and recruit further sales people. You need to widen your circle of influence. One of the ways of doing this is to make yourself more visible. Many direct selling companies do little if any media advertising. **Word of mouth, referrals, parties and showcases become the vehicles of extending the sphere of influence.**

You can create opportunities for yourself by participating in events where you can get greater exposure for yourself and your products to a wider range of people. Select a venue where you are likely to attract people who will need your products.

Here are a number of examples.
* **Bridal fairs** – cosmetics, glassware, costume jewellery.
* **School parent teacher associations** – encyclopaedias, children's books, children's toys and children's clothes.
* **School carnivals** – same as above.
* **Agricultural shows** – nutritional products, household products.
* **Social clubs** in corporations – cosmetics, jewellery.

Check with your corporate head office before you embark on outside marketing exhibitions. If your project is within the corporate culture, they will support you with brochures, extra display material and company props.

With all of these methods, the showcase, the party and a public display, the purpose is to reach a greater audience, bring your product to their notice and expand your market.

FUN WITH PARTIES

Helen Bruveris has written the ultimate guide to party plan selling. It is called **Party Your Way to Prosperity**. For an in-depth account of how to do it, Helen's book will prove invaluable. Most direct selling companies have a form of party selling as part of their direct marketing tactics. In the Mary Kay business they talk about a skin care class. In Nutri-Metics and Tupperware they have a **demonstration**, at Yves Rocher it is a skin care demonstration and at Jigsaw they have **a Talkabout**.

In most cases the concept is similar with a different focus. The party or demonstration serves three purposes. The first goal is to sell product to the women who attend. The second is to book **further parties from the group**, and the third is to **offer the business opportunity** to anyone present.

Having a party can be a fun experience for all those who attend. The success of the party will depend largely upon the organisation and the way you as the consultant run your party.

PREPARATION

- Organisation and planning are vital.
- Prepare your display material and products well before the party.
- When you start presenting parties, jot down the key points in your presentation in a written summary. Put in a folder with plastic sleeves.
- Confirm with your hostess a few days before the event that she has invited her guests.

THE EVENING OF THE PARTY

- Look smart, well groomed; wear something that is easy to move about in.
- Arrive at the hostess's home at least 20 minutes before the starting time to set up your display of products.
- Choose a well-lit space to set up your display. Arrange seating close by.
- Check to see if your visual aids are on hand.
- Ask the hostess for names and addresses of guests.
- Welcome the guests and initiate conversations with them when they begin to arrive. Give each guest a name tag.

THE PARTY BEGINS

1. Capture the attention of your audience.
2. Let your hostess introduce you, as the guests are her friends.
3. Do something to break the ice before you launch into a product presentation.
4. Share a story, play a game and brighten the atmosphere with a humorous anecdote.
5. **The Presentation.**
   - Thank the hostess and explain hostess incentives and gifts.
   - Introduce your company. Give a short history of the company, its philosophy and description of its marketing plan. This gives customers a sense of security about the reputation of the company.
   - Demonstrate the products.
   - Describe the benefits of each product.
   - Invite guests to examine and try out products.
   - Outline delivery and payment procedures.
   - Explain how to use order forms

- Highlight any special promotions.
- Sell the idea of a party date with a description of hostess gifts.
- Describe the business opportunity.
- Collect the order forms towards the end of the refreshment time. This gives women a chance to chat about their purchases. You can meet each woman one on one, offer some help and advice and extra product knowledge. **The business opportunity is the most valuable product you can help people buy.**

Make sure you can vary your sales pitch. During the closing remarks of a party demonstration, customers are invited to think about the prospect of having a party. The business opportunity itself should be the easiest product to sell. As Helen Bruveris says: "You are offering the security of self employment, the enjoyment of meeting many new people and of having fun on the job".

A demonstrator who recruits always seems to book more parties and achieve higher sales. The excitement of an active party generates enthusiasm, more activity and a positive, buoyant atmosphere.

TAKING ORDERS

Shopping time is when your creative sales ability will be put to the test. If you have presented your products with knowledge and enthusiasm your guests will enjoy buying them. **Book your parties first.**

Ask everyone if they would like a party and note those who say yes. Offer a choice of two dates and suggest setting a tentative date. Get them to write it in their diaries.

Invite your guests to talk about the business opportunity. Share your lifestyle and business success with your guests to focus on the advantage of working in their own time.

SELLING THE RANGE

The relaxed atmosphere of a home and group dynamics are extremely conducive to buying. You need to be **positive, enthusiastic and knowledgeable** about the products. A discussion about your customer's selection indicates you are interested in them. Include a door prize as an additional "present". Hand out order forms. Explain carefully how they are to be filled in. Discuss payment terms and delivery dates.

REFRESHMENT TIME

This should take place after the order time. You can let your hostess know the agenda for the party and give her an idea of the time you want her to serve coffee. If the guests decide to party on you can quietly excuse yourself. You don't have to be the last to leave. Thank everyone for coming and indicate you will contact them again.

THE PARTY FORMAT

Arrive 20 to 30 minutes before starting time.

Preparation Time 20 minutes	Set up your display Organise your brochures and handouts Speak with the hostess about refreshments Welcome the guests as they arrive
Presentation Time 30 minutes	Give a brief overview of company philosophy and hand out brochures Introduce hostess incentives Demonstrate the products
Shopping Time 30 minutes	Invite guests to be a hostess at their own party Discuss the business opportunity Help guests fill in order forms Explain delivery and payment procedures
Refreshment Time 30 minutes	Serve refreshments Finalise orders Confirm future party bookings Arrange for delivery and payment with hostess

Present your party with confidence and ease. After you have done a few parties you will become more comfortable with the pace and how much time to allow for each section. One and a half hours is ample time for the presentation, shopping and refreshments. For your own time frame add 30 minutes preparation time on to the program and travelling time to and from the venue.

A similar situation will exist with a beauty demonstration or a skin care class. Make sure everybody has fun and goes home happy with their purchases. **Most direct selling companies offer a money back guarantee which inspires customer confidence.** The object is to use the party as an effective sales arena to develop long-term customers.

Many women have never been invited to a direct selling party. The potential is therefore enormous. With many women handling full-time employment, their time for shopping is considerably reduced. A party combines a chore with an enjoyable social activity.

BENEFITS OF THE PARTY AS A MARKETING TOOL

FOR THE CONSULTANT
* The possibility of meeting new people, expanding your circle of influence.
* Quicker than doing one-on-one presentations.
* More sales generated through group synergy.
* In a recession, people might resist going shopping but will buy in a relaxed environment created at a party.

FOR THE HOSTESS
* An incentive gift.
* Some companies offer a percentage of sales to the hostess.

FOR THE GUESTS
* Service, ease of purchase and delivery.
* Facility to learn about products and a potential business opportunity.
* An enjoyable experience.
* Ability to make new friends.
* The possibility of becoming a hostess.

CHAPTER 10

THE POWER OF SHARING

Sponsoring

Networking

Learn to be Your Own PR

Organisations to Join for Networking

Role Models

SPONSORING

Direct selling is a people business. It grows through the **power of sharing** the business opportunity. Instead of hiding your business opportunity you go out of your way to expose it and share it. You have a range of products, you have a marketing plan to follow and a support system. All you have to do is extend the opportunity to other women who might be open, available and needing extra income. As we have said earlier, women became involved in this business for many different reasons and at different levels of motivation depending on their needs. All you need to do is offer to sponsor them. Show them the opportunity. They might not be receptive today or tomorrow but circumstances change and they might come back to you when their needs change.

Sponsoring is the process of sharing the opportunity someone else shared with you. Sponsoring is the lifeblood of your business. Your business needs two dimensions. One is selling the product and the other is recruiting others to sell the product.

BUILDING A NETWORK THROUGH SPONSORING

You can begin to build your own business by sponsoring as each personal recruit provides the potential for additional earning in your network.

Team building is your pathway for developing a real business where you can leverage your time. The more you sponsor, the more you can train and the greater your earning capacity. Your personal ability to sponsor is your best guarantee of success. Once you are actively sponsoring you can encourage your team to do likewise. Lead by example. Always be ready to share the opportunity with someone.

WHY SPONSOR?

If you rely only on your personal sales you will always be limited by your own time restraints. No matter how effective you are, you can only do a certain amount of personal selling. If however you build up a team, you can increase your earning power and your sphere of influence. Your business will gather energy, momentum and became a hub of activity which in itself is motivating and encouraging.

Your personal goals of acquiring a company car, a trip to seminars and other incentives depend on the performance of your team as well as your personal sales. The sooner you learn to sponsor, the sooner you can make these goals a reality for yourself.

Make sure you create the time each week to follow up leads of potential recruits. Set up sponsoring interviews. Make time to train new consultants. Analyse your work patterns. Make sure you invest a substantial part of your time in sponsoring activity and building a network.

DUPLICATION

Duplication comes from the Latin word, *duplicare* which means to double. The growth possibility in the direct selling business comes from duplication. One become two, two doubles to four, four to eight, eight to 16, 16 to 32, 32 to 64 and so on. Growth in your business will take on an unimaginable size if you keep duplicating. A sponsor must however take responsibility for the people she enrols and train, teach, nurture and support them until they are on the road to success.

HOW TO SPONSOR EFFECTIVELY

1. **Make a list of a minimum of 100 names.** Get out your personal phone book, your business card file and create a list. Think about people you have met through business, social activities, your children's school. Even if you think some of these people will not be interested in your business opportunity, still list them. Don't prejudge people.

2. **Prioritise your list.** Select high energy people. Choose positive people. List the successful people.

3. **Pick up the phone.** Call your prospects. Outline the reason for the call and arrange a meeting. Don't try and do a presentation on the telephone. Give the prospect a choice of two convenient times and set up a date.

4. Once you have had your meeting and shared the opportunity you need to arrange a time for **a follow-up call.** Keeping in touch is your best chance of success.

Your new recruit will first experience exhilaration, excitement and be very enthusiastic. She will tell some of her family and friends about the business. Some of the people she tells may sow the seeds of doubt in her mind. They could be cynical about it, they could make fun of the business. This wedge of doubt could cause her to quit before she starts.

PROTECT YOUR RECRUIT

It costs money, time and effort to recruit new prospects. In the first 72 hours after sponsoring a new distributor, it is up to you to protect your investment.

* Make sure you call your new recruit a few times in the first 72 hours.
* Prepare the distributor for some common negative reactions she might encounter from cynical outsiders.
* Provide the new distributor with some positive motivational material.
* Do not paint too rosy a picture when you recruit.
* Be sensible and realistic about the amount that can be earned.
* Go with your distributor to make her first presentation.
* Provide the new distributor with specific selling and recruiting techniques.
* If there are area rallies or meetings accessible to the distributor, do everything possible to get her to attend them.

Graeme Spry is one of Australia's foremost sponsoring experts. He says sponsoring is teaching, training, counselling, duplicating.

"We must become successful at sponsoring in order to build an effective network. Do not allow your new distributor to sponsor alone. Where possible present on a two-on-one basis with the new prospect which will eliminate **90 per cent** of sponsoring failures, providing **you know** what you are about," he says.

Some of Graeme's other principles are:

---

* Learn how to **show your marketing plan in five minutes.** No two-hour long presentations.
* Learn to teach, how to explain direct selling in an understandable, exciting and believable manner (in less than two minutes).
* Learn and teach listening skills, "How much does it cost to join?" You are not hearing a question which demands an answer in dollar terms. You are hearing, "I'm short of money".
* Find out why your prospect should become involved.
* What are your prospect's perceptions, needs, desires?
* Learn the turn-off words for a number of prospects such as door-to-door selling and pyramid and how to handle them.

WHAT IT MEANS TO BE A SPONSOR

A successful sponsor offers to help a new recruit set her business in motion. You need to share your time, your talent, your experience and your knowledge. You are both a mentor and a role model. **Encourage your new recruit to use and get to know the company's products as a first step in the process.** You will find recruits who adopt a negative attitude with comments like: "I can't find the time to get started" or "I lack confidence to get going".

We become successful when we take away excuses. Indecision and procrastination are the two worst enemies. Encourage your new recruit to begin NOW. I have written more about developing a team in the chapter on leadership, Taking Your Team To Success.

NETWORKING

Once you start following up on your list of 100 prospects, you will find some of the prospects will use your products, some will take up the opportunity and others will decline both. Some however will refer you to some of their friends. These referrals will be strangers you have never met before.

TALKING TO STRANGERS

Why does the idea of talking to strangers frighten so many people? We caution children in a protective way not to talk to strangers. As adults in safe environments, that caution is no longer valid.

The most amazing contacts I have made have come from talking to strangers. They did not remain strangers for long. Make friends out of strangers in
* Queues in banks, supermarkets and post offices.
* Elevators, trains, buses and waiting rooms.

MAKING FRIENDS

I would like to recommend **Andrew Mathews' Making Friends, a Guide to Getting along with People.** He tells us if you want friendship you must be a friend first. It is also about enjoying people. It is a light, easy to read book. Building a business is about making friends, building a team and getting along with people.

As John Kalench said: "The way to guarantee success in this business is to talk to more and more people. When you make a habit of making friends out of strangers, making money will become a habit with you. Make a game out of talking to strangers. I guarantee you will have a lot of fun and even more importantly you will have **made the world your oyster.**"

CREATING CONTACTS

To promote my first book, **There's a Lipstick in my Briefcase**, I did a lecture tour across Australia. I started in Perth and ended in Tasmania. I visited over 25 towns and cities across the country and I spoke to more than 10,000 women. In order to find groups of women I needed to effectively use the process of networking and actively follow up contacts. I met many women in the direct selling industry. **Direct selling is networking in action. Networking is the most effective method of sharing an opportunity.** I also discovered many different groups, societies and organisations of women who meet on a regular basis. I will share these contacts with you so you might use them to develop your networking business.

The opportunity for making contacts exists at every point in your day to day life. You can meet other women through your children's schools, charity organisations, professional clubs, sports activities, religious or church functions and in the process of doing your shopping, being at the hairdresser and socialising.

An openness to meeting people and making new contacts will not only enrich your personal life but will also give you a continuous bank of new women to whom you can sell your products, share the opportunity or just make friends.

Don't be afraid to approach people. All it takes is a smile, an opening statement and a little light chit chat to establish rapport. Take your business cards wherever you go. Remember you are not taking from someone, you are sharing an opportunity. You might think everyone you meet is aware of direct selling companies and your product in particular. However, this is not the case and many people will welcome the information you share.

LEARN TO BE YOUR OWN PR

When you are in business for yourself, as is the case in direct selling, it is important you are pro-active, take initiative and make it happen for yourself. You cannot sit behind your desk and make the phone ring. In direct selling you need to actively contact people to arrange your demonstrations, classes and parties. Tell people what you are doing. If you are in a cosmetic business, offer them a facial. Make yourself visible by sharing with others what it is you do.

MAKE A LIST OF PEOPLE YOU ALREADY KNOW

• Friends	• Your children's friends' mothers
• Family	• Sports contacts
• Husband's friends	• Hairdresser
• Office workers	• Receptionists
• Neighbours	• School PTA
• Church connections	• Clubs, classes

MARKET YOURSELF

In the direct selling business **you sell yourself first, then your company then your product.** People will buy from you if they like you. Being your own PR means you need to look the part at all times, have your diary and business cards on hand and always be on the look out for opportunities. One very good strategy in attracting attention for your product is to offer a free gift as a door prize at functions, in raffles and as part of other promotions. Cross promotions are an excellent way of getting increased visibility. Advertise in low-cost newsletters for your target market.

ORGANISATIONS TO JOIN FOR NETWORKING

Self development courses	Women and Management
View clubs	Zonta
International Training & Communication	Quota clubs
Business & Professional Women	Political clubs
Toastmasters	Australian Executive
SWAP (Salesperson with a Purpose)	Women's Network

SWAP is a wonderful organisation with branches in all metropolitan centres. Swappers meet once a week for breakfast with a guest speaker. Besides being a great opportunity to network, usually one has the privilege of hearing a wonderful motivational speaker. When I first went to SWAP meetings I thought SWAP stood for **Sex Without A Partner.** I arrived at 7am and found this group standing and thrusting their arms into the air with a hail and hearty, "I'm alive , I'm well, I'm feeling great". Inside me I thought I could not possibly participate in this exercise. I was invited as a guest speaker and there was no way I could appear stand-offish. I joined in. Doing it was definitely more comfortable than watching from the outside. Many meetings later I felt quite at home in this environment and began to enjoy the support and stimulation that the meetings provided.

In the appendix I have listed the addresses of some groups that are supportive, helpful and provide great opportunities to meet people.

Get your message to the market in simple, fun and low cost ways.

EFFECTIVE NETWORKING

* Always have your business card accessible.
* Follow up each contact with a phone call within a week.
* Always ask for the other person's card.
* If no card is available, have a pen to jot down telephone numbers.
* Don't trust your memory, write details down.
* Maximise your exposure at every function. Learn the art of mingling.
* Ask open-ended questions.
* Carry brochures of your product with you. Be a walking advertisement for your business.
* Go to company events.
* Use fun bumper stickers.
* Use buttons with messages eg. Herbalife's "If you want to lose weight ask me how".
* Create interesting business cards.
* Use cards, stickers, fridge magnets with your message printed on them

ROLE MODELS

The direct selling business has a unique quality: the built in facility of learning from role models. At whatever point you start there will be someone further along the road. You can learn from that person and they will support you in your endeavours. It will be in the interests of your leader to incubate your business, to show you the ropes and to support you in an active way. You will see living examples of successful achievers. Using some of their methods, combine these with your own personality, skills and experience.

CHAPTER 11

TAKING YOUR TEAM TO SUCCESS

PEOPLE MANAGEMENT

T he direct selling business is not only about selling and sharing the opportunity. It is essentially about multi-level management. We need to become great managers, wonderful team leaders and inspiring role models. We are not all born with the skills of managing a team however there is much we can learn and apply. In this business there is no point in being a **queen bee** and keeping all the glamour, glitter and glory for yourself. This is a business about sharing. A good leader has a solid sense of her own position and is not threatened or insecure about delegating and power sharing. The direct selling business is a people business. A company is only as good as its people. At Mary Kay, she regards her people as her most important asset.

Building a direct selling business is as basic as building a team. Successful leaders know how to create a loyal, enthusiastic and motivated team. I spoke to one of Australia's great team builders in the field of direct sales, **John Nevin.** For many years John was managing director of World Books. His strength was inspiring, teaching and supporting sales people. He shared with me some of his special secrets.

LOVE 'EM TO DEATH

John believes you need to treat your sales team as you would your family. You need to be with them in body, mind and spirit. You need to laugh with them, cry with them, sweat with them, stay up all night, work in the field and spend real tangible time with them.

He emphasises there are no short cuts. **A leader leads by example.** John does not believe you can be an armchair role model. You can't tell them how to sell. You **need to show** them by example. He also holds the notion that the leader needs to **feel passionately** about her business. This is what a team can emulate and internalise. He does not feel money alone motivates people. People work for many reasons, of which money is only one of them. They want to feel part of something and they want to achieve an identity. They want the feeling of belonging.

If you understand the reason for people working it makes handling them more effective. Make them feel **special**. Recognise birthdays, anniversaries and celebrate special occasions by sending them cards and gifts. Everyone is struggling for recognition and identity. Make sure you have a good reward system in place.

SECRETS TO TEAM BUILDING

- Love 'em to death.
- Treat them like family.
- No secrets, communicate fully.
- Open door policy, listen, be available.
- Spend time with team.
- Reward them publicly.
- Do not criticise your team.
- Show empathy.
- Maintain ethical standards.
- Have fun with your team.
- Hold frequent meetings.
- Lead from the front.
- Show them by example.
- Make them feel special.
- Build relationships with individuals.
- Give positive feedback.

KEYS OF LEADERSHIP

John Nevin also believes for a team to be healthy it needs to operate in a system of open communication. Secrets, in-fighting and politics have a negative effect on the morale of the team. Have many open discussions. He emphasised the need for frequent group get togethers about new products, promotions and innovative selling approaches. Daily training and daily meetings are a great way to keep momentum going. Have fun with your team. Make work seem like play.

- Management flows from leadership.
- Train your managers to be leaders.
- Give sales people product knowledge.
- Nurture your team.
- Teach them to set goals.
- Keep achieving your own goals.
- Share your own goals with them.
- Stimulate them with ongoing material, books, tapes, lectures, courses.

DRAMATISE

Great leaders have an innate ability to **communicate by actions** rather than by words. They dramatise.

Dramatise your message. Use role play, demonstrations, enact real life examples. Business is not only about facts. It's about **emotion, caring and passion**. It's about people. Your team wants to be inspired by you. The better you are as a role model, the more effective you will be as a leader. People trust good leaders when they perceive they are real – not facades.

BEING A GOOD LEADER

Effective managers know how to manage themselves first so both the people they work with and their organisation can profit from their presence.

One of the greatest qualities of good leaders is their ability to delegate. In order to delegate effectively, make sure you plan each day with a clear picture of what needs to be achieved and communicate this to your team. This planning needs to be done on a weekly, monthly and annual basis as well as part of an overall scheme.

The assets of a good leader	Demonstrate:
* Keeping cool in a crisis.	* Courage.
* Looking the part.	* Loyalty
* Efficient delegating.	* Integrity.
* Keeping your team happy.	* Wisdom.
* Taking initiative.	* Good values.

KEEPING COOL IN A CRISIS

When there are crises in the business, don't panic or get over-excited. Take cool, logical action. This self-discipline, in terms of emotional expression, is a valuable tool. Ask yourself questions to find out the extent of a crisis. How will it affect your profitability? What steps can you take to minimise the impact of the problem?

LOOKING THE PART

* You dress the part not only for outside impression but for your own team. They will have confidence in you if they sense you are in control of your image. **Part of looking the part is acting the part.**

- Don't bring your personal and emotional problems into the the relationship with your team. It is vital when you communicate with them that you are cool, calm and collected. Put any personal dramas at the back of your mind. This attitude has more than one benefit:
  - It acts like personal therapy, giving you a rest from whatever the problem is in your life.
  - Your team will feel secure when you present them with a calm exterior.
  - Find other people to share your emotional problems with.

BEING A FEMALE LEADER

A woman can bring special qualities to her role as leader.

* She can use her nurturing abilities to improve relationships within a team. She needs to be sensitive to any inter-personal conflicts within the team and anticipate personality clashes.

* She can display a caring attitude by listening to her team and suggesting realistic solutions.

* She can use intuition and perception to gain insight into problems. She also empathises with the needs of the working woman.

* She is more wary of politics in a team and is usually practical and down-to-earth with regard to problem solving. Most women dislike unnecessary meetings or bureaucracy as they need to come to grips with the job at hand and use time efficiently.

* She communicates more effectively, expresses more verbally and is generally more in touch with her own feelings.

* She acts as a role model.

* If you don't feel comfortable with the role of leader from the outset, act your role. Through doing it you will feel more at ease with it.

WOMEN CAN BE TOUGH AND TENDER

The effective manager combines the best of both male and female strengths. Women can be tough and tender, confrontational and co-operative. By combining such qualities women need to assimilate some of the traditional male managerial qualities into their style, such as the following:

- Risk taking – Women need to be more adventurous in trying new avenues and risking new styles of leadership.
- Women need to develop more control of their own emotions. They should be well prepared and appear competent and confident.
- Women need to accept responsibility and decision making as an integral part of their lives.
- Women need to be more objective and task oriented.
- Women should relinquish their need for perfectionism.
- In both business and personal affairs you need to know when you can lay your heart bare. A more guarded approach to exposing your soul is needed. A leader should keep her distance.

MOTIVATING OTHERS

Mary Kay, the founder of Mary Kay cosmetics, is one of the world's greatest female motivators. She believes in principles of integrity and honesty. She maintains if the business has a professional marketing plan, good products and an exciting remuneration and incentive program, everyone can be a winner.

Mary Kay often says in her book, **"the speed of the leader is the speed of the gang"**. She says people always resist change because it makes them feel insecure. If you as a leader include your team in the decision making they will be more supportive. People support what they help to create.

"Help other people get what they want and you'll get what you want," Mary Kay says. **"I wanted to create a company that would give women an opportunity to accomplish anything they were smart enough to do."**

Every sales director should be cheering for every woman in her team to succeed. No-one is afraid someone else will out perform them which is usually the case in corporate life. The more you assist your team to climb the ladder of success the more you will succeed.

Mary Kay believes her product will help other people by making them look beautiful on the outside which makes them feel beautiful on inside. She encourages her managers to project caring and genuine warmth. **"Set high standards, let people know you appreciate them."**

BE A FOLLOW THROUGH PERSON

Again borrowing from Mary Kay: **"Ideas are a dime a dozen but the men and women who implement them are priceless"**.

* Listen to their problems.

* Follow through with immediate solutions to problems.
* Develop trust.
* Never make a promise you can't keep.
* A manager or leader should never make a promise **beyond** her ability to keep it.
* Make sure you carry out your intentions.
* Don't leave your mail unanswered.
* Write down ten most important tasks to do tomorrow before you leave your desk today. Your list will keep you on track.
* Encourage your team to write everything down that requires follow through. Once on paper it becomes a tangible commitment.
* Regularly call consultants. Ask how they are and what they are doing.
* Regularly call your customers to check the products are working for them.
* Do your homework. Research a subject well.
* Have facts and figures at your fingers tips.
* Mondays are best days for sales meetings.

It is not necessarily the person with the most talent who excels but the person with **the most follow through**. The real achievers are those who follow through in all things big and small.

RUNNING AN EFFECTIVE MEETING

The basic aims of a meeting are:

* To motivate by setting goals.
* To develop skills.
* To share ideas and to brainstorm.
* To solve problems creatively.
* To provide fun and fellowship.
* To give information, communication.
* To recognise and reward achievement.

Request that each person takes notes. To lead the meeting you should be punctual, enthusiastic and make sure discussion does not get side-tracked. Irrelevant issues can be discussed on a one-to-one basis after the meeting. Listen attentively and make sure everyone gets an opportunity to contribute. Bring your meeting to a close by summarising the key points of your discussion.

PROCEDURE

Running a good meeting takes preparation, detailed planning and good organisation.

DO YOUR HOMEWORK

You have to sell ideas to gain the support of others. Do your homework for each meeting. Come up with thoughts, sayings and examples to inspire and motivate your group. Make it memorable.

BE ORGANISED

Have an orderly agenda. Keep notes, dates, a calender of events, results and proceedings of the meeting organised.

GIVE THEM SOMETHING

Make your meeting something to look forward to. Always make sure you have some special company news to excite your team. A new product, a new promotion or a seminar will make them very interested.

TIMING

Timing is important. Keep the meeting in a set time frame. Don't let it run longer than 90 minutes for the formal part.

AS A LEADER

It is your duty to keep the energy level up. Make sure there are no frequent interruptions which lose the focus of the meeting. **Singing songs unites people.** Use music and songs as they create atmosphere and team spirit. If someone is down, **music will lift the spirit**. No matter how you feel go in there with a smile. **Use humour.** The real test is to go in there and act as if all is well, when you have real personal problems. A well run meeting generates confidence in a leader's ability. **Enthusiasm** spreads like wild fire. If a leader is enthusiastic it is contagious.

Show depth of product knowledge. As a leader you need to be very well informed on the product development of your company, special offers, promotions and prices.

VENUE

When you start being a manager you might decide to have sales meetings in your home. As soon as your group is large enough select a more formal venue. This gives a more professional atmosphere to the meeting. **Choose a venue that has taste and class.** If you can use your corporate headquarters that is always a great advantage. If not select a venue and build up a good rapport with the function coordinator. If women go to an elegant smart venue, they feel good about their business.

MAKE A GOOD DISPLAY

Always take the trouble to make the meeting room look special. A display of products, flowers and whatever other touches you can add will enhance the visual effect.

REFRESHMENTS

I like the idea of serving refreshments afterwards. It creates a sociable and hospitable atmosphere. Tea, coffee and biscuits is all it takes.

DESIGN

Design the meeting for impact. **Create a warm, welcoming and exciting opening.** Make sure the middle flows with facts, figures, recognition and rewards. **Create a dramatic and theatrical close.** Leave them with something inspiring to last them for the week.

MONDAY SALES MEETINGS

Traditionally most direct selling companies have meetings on Mondays. To many people Monday signals the end of a carefree weekend and the beginning of a work week. "If last week was not good for you, it was good for someone else. **If you had a bad week you need the sales meeting, if you had a good week the sales meeting needs you.**"

Mary Kay says in her book on **People Management**, "I've been blessed with natural enthusiasm and this quality is responsible for my high energy level. I awake each day with renewed enthusiasm. I love what I do. Each day presents new opportunities to love and encourage each woman to success."

RECOGNITION

Praise symbolises recognition. Recognition and positive reinforcement are powerful motivators. Praise people to success.

INCENTIVES

Incentives are a very powerful motivator. Overseas trips, seminars, small gifts and even certificates give people an opportunity to be singled out and acknowledged. Little successes pave the way to bigger success.

The Mary Kay company gives pink cars and diamond jewellery as incentives. Nutri-Metics have white cars, gifts and overseas trips.

NEWSLETTERS

Newsletters can be used to praise individuals for achievement and to make people feel important. **People love seeing their name in print.** A newsletter gives you the opportunity to give recognition and information. Use photographs. Always recognise a spouse's contribution.

PERSONALISE

Personalising the business makes everyone feel appreciated.

BELONGING

Give each new director or manager a name for her team. Stargazers, Dazzlers, Sizzlers are fun names and are memorable and motivating.

DELEGATE PART OF THE MEETING

Don't try to run a one man show. Ask some of the consultants to do sections for you.

SALES MANAGEMENT

Sales management operates on many of the same principles as general team building with a slightly different focus. In a specific sales situation you need to:

- Give product information to your sales team.
- Make sure your team has samples and brochures.
- Give field training and occasionally go with sales people to observe their performance at shows and parties.
- Help your team set realistic goals. It is easy to put too much pressure on certain individuals.

Direct selling is essentially a people orientated business. The success of the leader depends on the personal success of each member of the team. **Take your team to success and you will be a winner.**

CHAPTER 12

TIME MANAGEMENT

Philosophy for Time Planning

Benefits of Time Planning

Secrets of Time Management

Setting Priorities

Planning

Activities in Direct Selling Business

The Paper War

PHILOSOPHY FOR TIME PLANNING

When I first started to read and analyse the subject of time planning, I was under the assumption I was dealing with a set of strategies and techniques. The deeper I delved the more I realised this was a very profound topic. It has its roots in our basic value system, our beliefs, our goals and our priorities.

I was under the impression time management was a set of techniques that enabled you to be on time for appointments. But this is not the purpose of time management. Nor is it designed to pile as many things as you can into each day. **Time planning teaches you to be effective.** It allows you to spend more of your time doing things that are of most value, whether it is work, building a business, being a mother, lover or friend or just having time to be yourself.

There is no way you can plan your day to day existence without knowing what you want to achieve in your life. First work out what you want, list your priorities and only then can you divide your day into manageable units.

Plan your time and you plan your life. Waste your time and you waste your life.

ENJOY BEING IN THE MOMENT

There is no point in planning for the future if you don't live the present moment. The point of planning is to free you so you can enjoy being in the moment. The idea is a little pre-planning will give you a smooth day that flows like a river. **Planning cuts out worry, anxiety and tension.** You know ahead of time you can meet deadlines, fit everything in and relax in the process.

Being able to control your time successfully also gives you a feeling of increased self-esteem. You feel good that you can **create a schedule and stick to it**. The process is positive, energising and gives you greater self con-fidence. You don't have the pressured feeling that everything is on top of you. The **experience of self-discipline**, of knowing you can set out a plan and accomplish it is rewarding and builds trust in yourself.

You also need to clarify your goals for yourself and get a clear picture of your values and priorities. What comes first for you? Is it your family, your work and then yourself? Put yourself first. **If you are calm, centred, con-fident and happy you can accomplish more in your business and give more to your family.**

CREATE MORE TIME

It is also possible to create more time. We all have the same 24 hours per day, seven days per week. How is it that the President of the USA can cope with 250 million people and we have trouble managing our little world? You can be innovative about how you use your time. **Have you ever thought about sleeping less?** Wake up one hour earlier every day and use that time for yourself – to read, meditate, exercise and walk. Use the time for yourself.

COMBINE ROLES

Combine roles and activities. Use meal times as a time to share with the family. Exercise with a friend or spouse so you can enjoy it together. Be creative about combining things you have to do with people you want to be with. Integrate all areas of your life.

In her book, **How to Get What You Want, Patricia Fripp** shares the following:

THINGS TO THINK ABOUT BEFORE SAYING YES.

1. Do I really want to do this?
2. Will those closest to me benefit?
3. Will I ever have the opportunity again if I don't take it?
4. Will I have to cancel other plans to make this commitment?
5. How much of my time will it take?
6. Will I benefit personally?
7. Will my business benefit?
8. How long will the task take?
9. How much energy will it take?
10. Be assertive and don't feel guilty about saying "no"

BENEFITS OF TIME PLANNING

* You will have more flexibility in your life.
* Control your time and you control your life.
* You experience less tension and stress.
* You accomplish amazing feats.
* You feel energised by completing tasks.
* You live in the moment.
* You have increased self worth and enhanced self-esteem.

SECRETS OF TIME MANAGEMENT

- Develop a written plan – keep revising it.
- Don't procrastinate – do it now.
- Do each task to completion with concentration.
- 80/20 rule. Spend 80 per cent of your time on tasks of high priority such as sponsoring and selling.
- Do high value actions first. Big jobs come first.
- Take one step at a time.
- Be proactive. Learn to say no when appropriate.
- Compartmentalise your projects.
- Know what you don't have to do perfectly. Don't try to be Superwoman.
- Delegate.
- Make an appointment to have time for yourself.

SETTING PRIORITIES

The more you have to do, the more you accomplish. You just get on with it instead of thinking about it. If you start the day with a list of ten things to do, by the end of the day if you have done all ten you'll feel great. Your energy level is directly related to the number of activities you complete in a day. Procrastination is de-energising.

Start the day with something you know you can complete. The rest of the day will flow in the same way.

PLANNING

Planning is the most important factor in structuring work priorities and integrating your business with domestic and family commitments. Achieving a perfect balance is often impossible. There will be periods of high business involvement when the domestic arena takes a back seat and vice versa. Expect these times to happen and flow with them.

To be organised you need to outline the various areas of your life and define all that needs to be done on a daily basis. **It is a matter of organisation and delegating.** The more organised the mundane aspects of life are, the more time you can spend with the people you love and the more time you will have for fun. Try to see your life as a whole and decide which functions you will do yourself and which services you will pay for. On a domestic level, divide up chores among all members of the family.

HOW TO PLAN YOUR TIME

*   Develop a system that works for you.
*   Analyse your tools of planning.
*   Stick to the system you use.
*   Keep one comprehensive diary or note book.
*   Write everything down in one book. Don't use bits of paper.

THINGS THAT DESERVE YOUR ENERGY

*   Will this increase my sales?
*   Can I learn from this? It is useful?
*   Is it beneficial to my family?
*   Is it fun?

TIME WASTERS

Identify your top time stealers. Ask yourself how many of them are in your control. Develop house rules so that your family respects your needs and priorities.
*   Keep things in the same place all the time.
*   Don't waste time on the telephone.
*   Television is a huge time killer.
*   Don't run out for single errands.
*   Shop once per week.
*   Put away unimportant tasks.
*   Schedule day dreaming for the bath, walks or while cooking.
*   Don't do for others what they can do for themselves.

WRITE EVERYTHING DOWN

I rely on lists, yet once the lists have been made they have a liberating effect. Tick off what you have done, and re-list the tasks still to be done. These lists include the following:

LISTS FOR ACTION

* Important business meetings in their appropriate time slot with the address and phone number of the venue in your diary. Jot down major points of discussion.
* Necessary phone calls to be made with the phone number written down next to it, name of contact, and subject of discussion.
* Tasks to be delegated.
* Personal errands such as doctor, dentist, hairdresser, library, shopping, dry cleaning, etc.
* Social commitments, seeing friends, birthday cards, gifts, entertaining, etc.

PACING YOURSELF TO REDUCE STRESS

* Make sure you give yourself time to plan.
* Exercise regularly.
* Meditate or practise relaxation techniques daily.
* Do some deep breathing.
* Balance your life between your needs, your work and your family commitments.

ACTIVITIES IN DIRECT SELLING BUSINESS

Analyse your business activities and make sure you allow adequate time for each function based on order of priority. Make sure no area is neglected, especially planning.

ACTIVITIES IN DIRECT SELLING

* Servicing customers.
* Local and interstate travel.
* Special events.
* Telephoning customers and team members.
* Planning.
* Financial management.
* Maintaining contact with your network.
* Marketing activities and networking.
* Promotional activities.
* General administration.
* Conferences, seminars.
* Doing presentations, parties.
* Sponsoring, one to one meetings.
* Training and teaching.

THE PAPER WAR

1. Handle every piece of paper only once. File it, bin it or respond to it immediately.
2. End each working day with a clean, tidy and organised desk.
3. Place completed projects in one folder and work in progress in another.

ORGANISATIONAL AIDS

- A big, one page per day desk diary.
- Page-a-day pocket diary.
- Notice board.
- Business cards filed in a unit.
- Alphabetical fax file/correspondence.
- Current projects in coloured folders.
- Source books.
- An up-to-date telephone directory and address book.
- Customer files.
- Filing cabinets.

CLEAR PLASTIC DISPLAY FOLDERS

It is important to have useful information at your finger tips if you want to work efficiently and effectively. Looking for things wastes lots of time. Keep material organised in folders as follows:

* Finance and bank statements.
* References, resumes, diplomas, certificates.
* Important documents such as leases, birth and marriage certificates, tax file number, bank account numbers, insurances, your will and any contracts.
* Company material, catalogues, promotions.
* Monthly magazines of company.
* Collect stories to use for presentations.
* Summary of training material.
* One master copy of articles written about your business.
* One master copy of each talk or presentation you have done.
* Inspirational sayings, words and material you can use for presentations.

CHAPTER 13

ROLE JUGGLING

Combining Roles of Mother and Business Woman

Secrets of Role Juggling

Superwoman is a Myth

Getting Balance in Your Life

Eliminating Guilt

Organise Yourself

How to get Husbands to Help

How to Make the System Work

COMBINING ROLES OF MOTHER AND BUSINESS WOMAN

I believe with great passion women are blessed and privileged to be able to juggle so many roles. Many of you reading this might think I'm out of my mind. How can this woman find something positive in the crazy juggling act that most of us have to perform? The secret lies in the contrast; the more roles you play the richer your repertoire becomes. **Each role nurtures, enriches and complements the other.**

We have to be mothers to our children, wives, role models, housekeepers, shoppers, nurse maids and taxi drivers. We are friends to our friends and as often as not we have extended family responsibilities, social, religious and community commitments besides our careers or businesses.

At the lectures I have given on business motivation, the most frequently asked question was how did I cope. There are effective tactics to change roles and to enjoy each role we play.

For most of us our motivation is the desire to **have it all**. We want a man, children, money, a career, friends, a life style, dreams and time to enjoy these things.

SECRETS OF ROLE JUGGLING

QUIT WORRYING and get organised. It seems like a contradiction, but the more you plan and the more organised you are, the more able you are to live in the moment. If you have worked out an action plan for the day you can let it unfold.

Schedule some time for yourself: first to spoil yourself and second to plan. It is often better to stop in order to plan than to rush around. My mother was always so busy she did not have time to do things that were really important to her. She did not have a career or a business. She was busy being busy and always said she didn't know where the time had got to.

Have you noticed how successful people always have time if you need them? They accomplish all they need to. **They use time as their resource.**

The more roles you juggle, the more skills you acquire. Busy women do things quickly, they don't fuss and they know how to keep more than two balls in the air at once without fear of dropping one. Women have learned to take on a variety of business tasks by effectively managing their personal and domestic lives.

SUPERWOMAN IS A MYTH

As the writers **Sokol and Carter** point out: "Smart women know ... you cannot have everything – at least not at the same time. Superwoman is SUPER-TIRED."

If we try to do everything at the same time something is going to get short changed. It will probably be, our needs.

We all bought the 1980s myth of superwoman and wonderwoman rolled into one. She lives an incredibly happy life in an incredibly beautiful home with her incredibly successful, supportive and handsome husband and their two adorable tots. She's not me. She's not you. She doesn't seem to be any of our friends. So who is she? Where is she?

We need to learn not to do things perfectly. Decide what is important and do it well. Don't torture yourself with being a super-wife, super-success and super-mother.

The truth is that being married, having children, building a business and staying sane in the process is an extraordinary juggling act. We cope some of the time. We get stressed a lot of the time. We never have enough time to do all the things we need to and very few of the things we want to. We are always last on the list. Having special, quiet peaceful time to indulge ourselves becomes the greatest luxury.

But there are short cuts, tips and tricks that will make your day work for you. You cannot put more hours into the day but you can use more of your time doing the things that matter most to you.

Time is the greatest resource you have. Waste your time and you waste your life!

CAN WOMEN HAVE IT ALL?

Women are asking for help. They are frustrated, tired, burnt out and carrying around loads of guilt. They want a career. They want success. But they won't pay the price of sacrificing marriage and children.

Women have real concerns about how to manage a career, family and marriage without sacrificing something. At all of my talks, question time invariably gives rise to the inevitable: "Are you still married to the same man? How did your husband cope? Did your marriage survive?"

My marriage did not survive. However my career was not the cause of its failure. At various times women do have to make sacrifices. The key is to keep your priorities in your mind.

MARY KAY STRATEGY

Mary Kay in her bestseller, People Management shares a very simple strategy:

1. List your six most important tasks.
2. Put them in order of importance.
3. Start with item No.1 on your list.
4. Cross off each item as you complete it.
5. Finish each task properly.
6. Re-enter any item not completed on next day's list.

This is a simple, easy to follow technique. Do it. It will force you to focus on your priorities each day, get them done and move on.

GETTING BALANCE IN YOUR LIFE

Being happy and fulfilled is a matter of combining the things you need to and love to do. It is the blend and balance of the elements that create a full and challenging existence.

It is healthy to feel tired after a busy day. But stress and frustration are de-energising and debilitating. How do you get to feel the healthy tired?

Balance lies in the combination of your roles and activities. You need to decide what these are. For each of you this balance will be a different recipe.

Make sure your home remains a haven for yourself and your family. If you have no time to get the housework done, **get someone else to do it.**

MAKING TIME FOR FRIENDS

A woman's friends are much more than her social life. My girl friends are my support group, my **confidants, my pillars of strength**. It takes a long time to develop good friendships and it is important to **nurture, cherish and keep sharing** with friends to keep the relationships alive.

The busier your life is, the less time you have for arrangements and friends. Here are some of the special activities I share with friends. **Create your own schedule** for time with friends.

* Two calls per day to chat.
* At least two meetings a week with two different friends which might be a half-hour coffee break or a quick shared lunch.
* I go jogging with a friend twice per week at 7am.
* I walk with another friend once a week.
* Once a month I take off a Saturday afternoon and go to an art exhibition or a movie with a friend.

ELIMINATING GUILT

Guilt is a very destructive emotion. It serves no positive purpose. It undermines your self-esteem. If you do something you don't feel happy about, acknowledge it, take responsibility for it and move on. Prolonged guilt is poisonous and will begin to destroy your inner being.

LEARN TO SAY NO

The way you spend your time is a result of how you manage your priorities. **Stephen Covey** in his brilliant book, **The Seven Habits Of Highly Effective Men** talks about using your values and principles as a base for making decisions on how you use your time. It is much easier to say no if you are clear about your priorities.

DON'T TRY TO BE PERFECT

Know when enough is enough. A smart woman knows it is not important to have shiny floors and a spotless house. This is not your ultimate goal in life. Accept imperfections and use your energy in achieving the goals that really count.

DECIDE WHAT YOU REALLY WANT

Once you decide on your priorities it is easy to know where to put your time, effort and energy. If your marriage is your most important relationship, that is where you invest most of your time. There are times when you will refuse career opportunities in favour of being with your children and other times you will miss an important school function because you are away on business.

Get in touch with yourself, work out your priorities.

HAVING A ROLE MODEL

My own mother stayed at home and was a full-time mother for 25 years. At the end of it all she still felt guilty and unfulfilled. She started to develop a career for herself at 45. She became passionate about her work, excited and confident. I have a number of aunts who were role models for me: one was a politician, another became an foreign diplomat and one was a businesswoman. Women who have accomplished this can share with us the **compromises, trade-offs and strategies** that enabled them to succeed.

ORGANISE YOURSELF

The key to good organisation is **LISTS**. I have a business action plan, a home list and a long-range goal list. Each night before I go to sleep I check off my priorities. The minute you have a list you are in control. Each time you cross something off you sense a feeling of achievement.

CREATE A NETWORK

You all need people who can **help in emergencies**. Keep an active list of repairmen, plumbers, electricians, mechanics, vets, doctors and babysitters as well as friends who will help in an emergency.

DELEGATE

Get a cleaning service or housekeeper. I do not see any virtue in housework especially when you can afford to hire help. Household help can make all the difference. Don't do things others can do.

PUT YOURSELF FIRST

Do what you want to do. Do what makes you happy.

Every day you are confronted with the need to compromise. If you can make a choice in the light of what you want, you are in control of the choice. Don't make moves in the spirit of sacrifice, that only leads to resentment.

Every woman should be able to earn a living and make herself financially independent. Not every woman wants to juggle full-time motherhood with a full-time career but it is important to have the inner feeling that you could if you had to. **Direct selling gives you an opportunity of having a flexible life style.**

GETTING DOMESTIC HELP

Make a list of the routine tasks that have to be done each day and **check off the ones that nobody else can do for you.** Decide together with your partner what he is prepared to tackle. Know what you want to do and delegate the balance. Children are also able to undertake small responsibilities.

Having a cleaning service has been great for me. I will encourage other women to do the same. Imelda Roche, the chief executive of Nutri-Metics emphasises the importance of encouraging women to get paid help as soon as their direct selling business allows them to afford it.

GROCERY SHOPPING

Do your grocery shopping once a week. Most women shop too often. Shopping once a week saves time and money. Make a list and pin it to your grocery cupboard. Add to it. Take the list with you once a week.

QUICK MEALS

My policy is to spend no more than 20 minutes preparing the evening meal. I enjoy that 20 minutes as I find it absorbing and relaxing. I know many women would rather spend a few hours cooking on the weekend and reheat the prepared meals in the microwave. I use only one pot dishes. This saves time in washing too many pots and kitchen utensils. I also buy some wonderfully prepared pasta sauces and desserts which saves on the fiddly bits when entertaining.

HOW TO GET HUSBANDS TO HELP

There are the rare men who will do more than take out the garbage ... and then there are the others. How can you get your man to handle some of the chores and share household responsibilities? Here are some of the secret tips I have learnt.

Use positive reinforcement. Positive reinforcement is **hugging your husband** if he does a load of laundry. Conversely, negative reinforcement is telling him he used too much detergent.

When my son was two weeks old my husband changed the baby's nappy. Instead of praising him I made a fatal mistake. I told him he'd put the pin in at the wrong angle. He never changed another nappy. I killed it for myself.

The wise woman will **cultivate a blind eye for imperfection.** Compliment him on a job well done. Don't give positive reinforcement every single time. It would appear too obvious. Just give occasional doses. Praise and appreciation engenders good will and co-operation.

One of my friends had four children fairly close together. She solicited her husband's help in the evenings while she breastfed. His job was to bathe the toddlers and fix dinner. Her eldest has just turned 22 but her husband still thinks she is breast feeding! She is not about to dispel the illusion.

IS MARRIAGE THE SALT OF DAILY LIFE?

Many women have tried marriage and decided it does not work for them. Others who are happy in a marriage would say it is the best thing in their lives. Out of my seven closest friends at age 40, three are still married to their first husbands and happy, three are divorced and one is blissfully remarried. What do the three who are still married have that is so special they are prepared to make their marriage a priority in their lives? Real love is the result of trust, compromise and commitment.

Traditional roles and responsibilities are no longer viable.

You have to negotiate a new relationship for yourself.

HOW TO MAKE THE SYSTEM WORK

For a system of shared responsibilities and delegation to work you need:

- **Communication** – Regular communication with your partner is important in a dynamic relationship. Make sure you explain all things clearly.
- **Regular talks with your children** – You might go for a walk with each child individually. Spend separate time together where you can really talk to each other.
- **Assertiveness** – Once you have delegated functions assert yourself if someone is copping out or not doing what is required of them. There is no point in an elaborate organisation if no-one adheres to the schedule.
- **Keep cool in crises** – Dramas do happen and they will descend on you when you least want them. Encourage a non-panic reaction in your family and action oriented responses.
- **Personal flexibility** – Be resourceful in solving problems.
- **Write down all instructions** – Keep a very large, visible notebook containing all relevant information.
- **Keep the house organised** – Everyone should know where to find tape, scissors, bandaids, spare cash, emergency phone numbers etc. Always put things back in the same place.

STRATEGIES FOR JUGGLING ROLES

- Delegate.
- Learn to say "no".
- Be organised.
- Eliminate guilt.
- Know your priorities.
- Don't try to be perfect.
- Make trade-offs.

- Make compromises.
- Put yourself first.
- Get your husband to help.
- Make time for friends.
- Get paid help.
- Create a network.

CHAPTER 14

RAISING POSITIVE CHILDREN

RAISING POSITIVE CHILDREN

T he best way to raise a positive kid is to start by becoming a positive parent."

The only qualification I have in writing this chapter is that I feel I have raised two happy, healthy, well adjusted, motivated kids. I will share with you what has worked for me. I'm also convinced the only way to raise positive kids is to start by becoming a positive parent. We can choose to adopt an optimistic view of life. Before you can positively parent your children you have to make and live that choice.

I went to university and majored in child psychology. I read and studied every theory from Freud to Erikson. Each time I uncovered more revelations I would rush home to my mother and tell her where she had gone wrong in bringing me up.

I was 23 when my own baby Jason was born. I was convinced the baby was right about everything and I had no confidence in my own ability to respond. I let him demand feed. I ended up feeding every hour instead of every four hours. He never slept through the night until he was three. He had amazing temper tantrums. I used to pretend he didn't belong to me when he lay on the floor of Woolworths supermarket and screamed. By the time he was two, I also had a six-month-old daughter, Nikki. She was doing her fair share of not sleeping. I was a zombie. It seemed there would be no life beyond dirty nappies, sleepless nights, musical beds, breast feeding, stained bras and being constantly on the go. I was frazzled. My own boundaries had dissolved.

That was when I asked the advice of a friend who had seemed to stay sane through three children. She said I had to separate from my eldest child, to redefine my own boundaries and to teach him the limits. I started to return to sanity. I didn't love the child any less but I let him know there were times I closed the door and he did not have access to me.

All my text-book psychology did not prepare me for real life motherhood. I learnt on the job and from other mothers. I decided I did not want to be a negative punishing mother. I did not believe you could spoil a child under three with too much love and once I had combined the love with some limits I think I had the perfect recipe.

SELF-IMAGE

One of the most important qualities the truly successful person must have is a healthy self-image. What chance do children have of developing a good self-esteem unless their parents have a positive self image?

Some of the causes of poor self-image in kids are
* Child abuse.
* Abandonment.
* A family where one parent suffers from alcoholism or drug addiction.
* A traumatic divorce.
* Over critical parents.

CHILDREN NEED UNCONDITIONAL LOVE

We need to love our children unconditionally, that is without any prior conditions. A child's self-image is to a large degree dependent on how he thinks you, the parent, really feels about him or her.

1. Understand and accept your children for what they are.
2. Help your children develop an enthusiastic outlook on life. Give them hope, optimism and faith in the future.
3. Encourage your children to complete tasks no matter how large or small. This develops self-esteem.
4. Stimulate your children to read and love books.
5. Build your children's self-image by teaching them manners, social graces, table etiquette.
6. Emphasise your child's creative imagination.
7. Help your child accept himself in a non-critical way.
8. Reward, praise and encourage where you can.
9. Establish a positive loving environment. Give frequent affection, put your arms around them, hug and kiss them, tell them you love them.
10. Encourage a spirit of excellence. Live your life in the same spirit. There is no integrity if the child does not learn from the positive example of the parents' behaviour. It's up to parents to act out what they teach their children. **Encourage your children to be the best they can.**

MOTIVATION

In order to raise positive kids, you need to motivate them. Motivation is something you instil on a regular basis. Just as you won't hear one speaker and expect to benefit from the effects for the rest of your life, your children need continual regular positive input.

Don't give your children mixed messages. It causes confusion. Clarify your own values. Let your philosophy about life show in your actions. What are your priorities? If you spend all your time playing golf or watching television, this is what your children see.

Don't expect teachers to be responsible for developing children's self-esteem. Parents must take responsibility.

LISTENING TO YOUR KIDS

Kids want our undivided attention. The key ingredient in family communication is **to listen** to what is being said. Most families do not communicate, they simply live in the same house. We have to learn to set aside quiet time to listen and to be there for our children.

Last year my 16-year-old son Jason, went to a wonderful camp called Discovery. There he learnt a number of skills. One of these involves a red velvet heart that fits in the palm of your hand. If you have something special to discuss, you hold the heart and speak. The other person listens. Then the process is reversed. It forces you to be attentive and listen. The heart is kept in a special place. When your child has something special to discuss or share, he or she brings the heart to you as a signal. **Mum, this is time for a heart-to-heart.** The process stops you from shouting, interrupting and limiting the discussion. It forces you to LISTEN.

DISCIPLINE

"Let the 'no's' be few but consistent and with love."

I was brought up by a very strict mother. "No" was the word I heard most often. I experienced childhood as a restrictive prison. I reacted by becoming a rebel and a non-conventional adult. Although I was given lashings of love and care, I felt stifled by all the restrictions imposed on me. As an adult I began to understand the no's were an expression of my mother's fears.

I believe children need limits and boundaries but I find having a few rules rather than many is far more effective. The rules changed as my kids grew up but I always found them to be co-operative and respectful towards the few rules we had. Children need simple and consistent rules. Until the age of 11 a child needs to learn by concrete example.

"Tell me, and I'll forget
Show me and I may not remember
Involve me and I'll understand."
– Native American saying.

HOW TO HANDLE CONFLICT

There are often situations where children are tired and hungry. Mothers too, are tired and under pressure. The combination causes an explosion. The children react by shouting, screaming and fighting. The mother loses her temper, smacks them and everyone ends up even more upset.

You should respond differently. Either take a few deep breaths and walk away from the commotion or hug and soothe the children and try to calm them down.

The first time we had a heart-to-heart, my son asked me to cancel a speaking engagement so I would be in town for a special event he wanted me to share. All I could think of was the sales I would miss, the business opportunity lost. I stormed out into my car and drove and drove. I was upset and tearful. I parked next to the sea, put the radio on and howled. When I was ready to drive home, my battery was flat. I had also left home without my purse. I sheepishly had to call my son and ask him to get the NRMA. It was a freezing winter's night and I was miles from anywhere. I came home feeling very embarrassed about my behaviour. I didn't go to my speaking engagement. I went with him to his function. I was forced into evaluating my behaviour and was able to effectively resolve the conflict.

QUALITY TIME

Love for a child is spelt T-I-M-E.

All children need to feel loved from the beginning. The best way to show love is by spending time with a child and enjoying the process. Although I was very busy with two businesses when my children were little, I made the time available. At bedtime, for 30 minutes we would read stories together. Every Friday we would go to the library. Each child would get two books. Each evening I would read to them. It was also a time for cuddling, hugging, tickling and "being loved". That worked for me with my two little ones who are 20 months apart. Now, many years later that time investment has paid dividends.

Real quality time is doing things together and side by side. No matter how busy I was, I maintained a few special traditions in our home. I had people to dinner once a week. The purpose of this was to make our home a place where people came, a centre of hospitality and warmth and a place where we gave generously of ourselves to others. Our home was always a place where friends popped over for coffee and cake. I wanted to show the children by example.

Once a week on a Saturday afternoon I would have a "bake in" with the kids. We would make oat cookies, cheese cake, fudge or something fun.

They would do it with me: taste it, lick the bowls and help. There would be flour, sugar and dripping chocolate all over the kitchen. We would take our fresh baking for a picnic tea somewhere special. Saturday afternoon was for them.

At other times our lives had to run like clockwork, schedules were organised, baby sitters and bedtimes. The routine gave them predictability and security.

LET THEM LEARN BY EXPERIENCE

I also believe in keeping cool in a crisis. If a mother panics children become frightened. Whatever drama erupted, rule No. 1 would be to keep cool, deal with the emergency without getting hysterical. Do not magnify the situation. This has stood them in good stead as young adults. They don't lose control and become frightened when unexpected things happen.

My mother always reminded me that children don't ask to be born. They are your responsibility until they are independent adults.

My experience and knowledge of children has been developed as a student of psychology, as a mother and as a teacher of art to children for more than 20 years. When children first come to my art class I tell them there is no such thing as a mistake: "We won't be using erasers in this class. If you draw or paint something you have to solve your problem in the painting."

Creating pictures is a parallel to life. If we make a mistake, we can't rub out what we have done. We have to work our way out of a situation. I encourage children to explore creative solutions. When they first come they are terrified. They are inhibited. They are scared of making a mistake. At school they are constantly in a position of fear. What's going to happen to them if they get something wrong? After a time, they realise it's not so difficult to explore solutions. In fact it's fun. The fear of punishment is removed. I tell them whatever they draw or paint is acceptable. It does not have to look like anything real. They gradually gain their confidence. In all situations we need to let them learn by experience, to let them try without fear.

PARENTS AS ROLE MODELS

Being a parent is an awesome responsibility. **The difficult part is you only get one go at it.** As the experts say **it's simple but it's not easy** to be patient and consistent. We get so involved in the minutiae of each day.

When my kids were little their father was studying medicine for seven years. I ran a business from home. They accepted Dad's study and Mum's work as reality. Later on when he graduated and found a job, we both had to do a certain amount of business travel. We decided one of us would always be at home with the kids. We became known as the yo-yo family one in, one out. My object was to keep my children feeling secure, safe, in a routine and centred in their world.

HUMOUR HELPS, TRY IT

As Zig Ziglar said: "To maintain an optimism and increase our chances for raising positive kids, we must have a sense of humour to overcome the problems, obstacles and discouragement we all confront from time to time. **Help your child develop a sense of humour.**"

I try and show my kids the funny side of serious situations. Many scenarios are potentially sad but if you can see the humour you get another perspective. Laugh a lot. Look at the lighter side. **Smile when you see your children first thing in the morning and last thing at night.**

CREATE A LOVING ENVIRONMENT

The beginning and end of each day are very important for children. Help your children start and end the day in a loving, optimistic way. If you wake your child with a gentle kiss, something to drink and warm words, they will enter the day in a positive mood. Until my children were about eight I used to end their day with two stories, a hug, a kiss and some time just sitting on their bed without hurrying away. A child needs to know he is special.

Many **million children go to bed hungry for food.**

Many more children go to bed **hungry for praise and appreciation.**

WHAT CHILDREN NEED TO SURVIVE A WORKING MOTHER

*   Love, lots of it.
*   Security.
*   Stability.
*   Consistency.
*   Stimulation.
*   Nurturing – taking care of their needs.
*   Positive self-esteem – approval. Praise teaches children to say "I can".

Words To Use With Your Children As Often As Possible

Super	Wonderful	Sensational
Great	Remarkable	Terrific
Fine	Excellent	Outstanding
Marvellous	Congratulations	Fantastic

> **Positive Phrases**
>
> | | |
> |---|---|
> | Good job | That's your best ever |
> | Well done | You are improving |
> | That's good | Nothing can stop you now |
> | Keep it up | You are on the right track |
> | I'm proud of you | Beautifully done |
> | I'm glad I'm your mum | You are a joy |
> | You are learning fast | |

WORKING MOTHERS NEED TO

* Plan quality time with their children.
* Decide on priorities.
* Get good help, child care and support.
* Create a secure, predictable environment.
* Tell children what's going to happen.
* Keep cool in crises.
* Give kids lots of affection – hugging and kissing.
* Keep rules and restrictions to a minimum.
* Know discipline is healthy and good.

BENEFITS OF A WORKING MOTHER

Children can thrive with a working mother because:

* Mother is alert, alive and stimulated.
* Mother has better self-esteem, this is catchy.
* Her interests, career and associates broaden a child's life.
* Child's life has to be well organised, this gives the child security.
* Children learn about real life.
* Parents set the example – success is a great example.
* Actions speak louder than words for inspiration.

SPECIAL ACTIVITIES TO DO WITH CHILDREN

* Fun outings.
* Time to be quiet together.
* Time to play together.
* Walks in nature.
* Reading books together.
* Listening to music.
* Spiritual togetherness.

RAISING POSITIVE KIDS IN A NEGATIVE WORLD

My children are my inspiration and my reason for being. For them I would climb Everest, swim the Nile, reach for the stars. My children are the source of my deepest joy. Their happiness and success is my ultimate goal.

I strongly believe children benefit the most when their mother is involved in a career which gives her self-confidence and greater self-esteem. As you will see when you read the interviews that follow, each mother says her success has spread to all other areas of her life. Their children are proud of their mums' successes, it broadens their world and they get increased positive input.

My daughter, Nikki was the model on the packaging of my toy products. Six weeks after emigrating to Australia, her face was on the shelves of toy shops and department stores. This brought her instant fame and recognition. It was good for her self-esteem. I have always believed it is valuable to involve your children in your business as much as possible.

"If a child lives with approval he learns to like himself. If a child lives with security he learns to have faith."

CHAPTER 15

HANDLING HUSBANDS

Equality in Marriage

Sell Him the Benefits of Your Business

The Secrets of Working Together

Intimate Relationships

Perfect Partnerships

KAREN AND RON BRADY, Nutri-Metics

SANDY AND KEN MCDONALD, Nutri-Metics

DEANNA AND MICHAEL PURZA, Nutri-Metics

TRACEY AND LEON WAXMAN, Nutri-Metics

FREDA AND WAYNE LAWRENCE, Rawleigh

SUE AND BRIAN UPTON RICHMOND, Le Reve

MARIA AND TED LEE, Pro-Ma Systems

MARIE AND DAVID WORDEN, Aloette

HANDLING HUSBANDS

EQUALITY IN MARRIAGE

As Harriet Lerner says in her book, **The Dance Of Intimacy**: "Intimate relationships cannot substitute for a life plan, but to have any meaning at all, **a life plan must include intimate relationship**".

I believe in order for women to make changes in their lives and feel equal in a relationship they need to have the same resources at their disposal as men. Up to now, women have not been encouraged to put energy into developing economic independence. The role of homemaker places women in a position of vulnerability. Given the current divorce rate, low or uncollectable childcare payments, it is no wonder the **poverty rate of single mothers is increasing.** The only course of action is for women to develop their **own financial resources.** They do not need to put 100 per cent of their energies into their career 100 per cent of the time. However a woman needs to have a **life plan of her own** that not only enables her to earn a living but to **find fulfilment outside of her marriage.**

Men are starting to see the value of women being able to take care of themselves financially. Women earning can relieve some of the strain on men. I have always felt sorry for men going out there to earn alone. A shared responsibility is a much more realistic solution.

Women want men to share in domestic chores and parenting. To help change men's attitudes women must reframe traditional expectations. Women must remove any threats and fears men may have about their wife earning and being independent.

SELL HIM THE BENEFITS OF YOUR BUSINESS

If your husband is not yet supportive of your direct selling business, you need to clarify for him the benefits you can both experience.

* Personal growth.
* Increased income.
* A more exciting life style.
* Overseas seminars for both parties.
* A possible company car.
* The challenge of building a business.
* Sharing the financial burden.
* Stimulation of meeting new people.
* Less financial pressure in the family.

Include him in what you are doing. Take him along to meetings, share your achievements and your goals. Discuss ways of doing it with him. Plan your long term financial goals. Let him see the benefits of your not being helpless, hopeless and financially dependent.

Most companies stress that a woman should not put her business before her husband. The philosophies of the companies I spoke to all said family before business.

Most companies acknowledge and reward husbands for their part in the wife's achievement and give recognition to both partners. The reason for this is that to be successful a woman needs her partner's support. If a husband is encouraging and supportive towards his wife's business, this gives her the impetus to develop further. Negative husbands undermine the positive effects generated by the business. Many women said their husbands were indifferent until they saw lots of money coming in, tangible rewards which showed that this was a "real business" opportunity.

THE SECRETS OF WORKING TOGETHER

I spoke to many couples about running their direct selling businesses together and found many combinations of talents. Claire Roche, daughter of Bill and Imelda Roche founders of Nutri-Metics Australia said of her parents: "**Dad is the visionary.** Mum takes his ideas and makes them happen. Dad is the financial planner, but Mum takes care of bottom line profits. Dad organises production, package design and administration. Mum is brilliant with people. She handles all the sales and marketing." In this marriage, we see how a couple can divide their functions according to their strengths.

John and Sherien Foley who have been executive directors for Pro-Ma Systems for more than seven years, also work together. **John loves organising the big events, seeing the big picture.** Sherien spends a lot of time nurturing and developing women and giving them counselling and guidance.

Naomi and Roger Alberts have also combined their talents and respective strengths. **Roger is a brilliant speaker and presenter.** Naomi is a wonderful one-on-one communicator and stays close to the product.

Stuart and Beth Carseldine, Amway Executive Diamonds, also combine their talents to run a very successful business. Stuart is the go-getter. He works with the movers and shakers. Beth is the listener. She counsels the newcomers as they find their feet. **Stuart "motivates the socks off the audience".** Beth tells them how it really is for her. Her honesty wins many hearts, much loyalty and a great following.

The secret is to each use your strong points, give each other space and work with a unity of mission and goals.

- Make your partner feel special and wonderful.
- Schedule quality time together.
- Share your business goals.
- Share business functions and responsibilities.
- Combine talents, business skills and energy.
- Support each other.

The husband's presence makes other men feel more comfortable about direct selling as a business.

CAN A RELATIONSHIP SURVIVE WORKING TOGETHER

The problem with building a business together is the constant proximity and interaction and the lack of space for the individual.

If a relationship is good, with care it can withstand the pressures of working together. Fortunately in the direct selling business you don't have to contend with being in a confined space like a shop, day in, day out. You can divide and share the business tasks.

Women need to ensure they are an integral part of the financial decision making of the business. It is not healthy for the woman to be "in business" but not active in making business decisions, dealing with finances and in a role where she has no real power. As a couple sort out your functions according to your strengths. **Create autonomy and space within your roles in the business.** This independence will give you both breathing space.

INTIMATE RELATIONSHIPS

"The highest goal of a relationship is to allow the other person to become the best person they can be."

What do we need in a relationship to make it intimate?
* A clear sense of self.
* Clarity of purpose and a life plan for each.
* The ability to communicate.
* Knowledge of your own values and principles.
* The ability to express your own feelings.
* Confidence to set boundaries.
* The belief that you can grow together.
* The willingness to share each other's goals.
* Accepting the other person without wanting to change them.
* Being able to resolve conflict.

FUN AND ROMANCE

We also need romance. I'm a great romantic and I believe there is a yearning and a need in most men and women to experience passion, poetic ecstasy and lovemaking which is fun, creative and relaxing.

In pursuit of enhancing our sexual relationship I encouraged my man to purchase a book called **How to satisfy a woman every time... and have her beg for more! The first and only book that tells you exactly how.** I was very excited when I found the book. I expected new heights of passion, ecstasy and excitement. We read the book together. By the time I had read aloud to the end of Chapter Three I think my partner was feeling permanently impotent. He found this the most threatening, invasive and traumatic information. I quickly dismissed the book as nonsense and resurrected his ego as only a woman knows how.

Set aside time for fun, cuddling, doing special things together and creating an environment where you do feel like physical intimacy. Busy lives, bustling households, sleepless nights, business demands all combine to destroy intimacy romance and fun. **It is up to you as a woman to make this an important element in your life for the benefit of both of you.**

HANDLING THE MALE EGO

According to your strengths, a couple should look at administration, financial management, sponsoring, sales and supporting functions to see who is best suited to the various tasks.

The essential differences between male and female, especially in their communication styles, make it difficult for men to express their feelings, frustrations and fears. Despite the risk of militant feminists tearing me apart, I **believe women can take care of the fragile male ego in special ways.**

* Don't belittle him.
* Don't be over critical.
* Give appreciation and praise where you can.
* **Make him feel as if he is the most wonderful lover in the world.** (Whether he is or not.) He does not know the truth and never will.

FROM THE COVER OF VOGUE TO INTERNATIONAL ENTREPRENEUR

KAREN AND RON BRADY
NUTRI-METICS

Karen is the Grace Kelly of Nutri-Metics. At 53, she is still an incredibly beautiful, gracious and elegant woman. She was born in northern NSW and has been married to Ron Brady, a former Queensland TV personality, for more than 30 years. They have a daughter and a son and have been involved with Nutri-Metics since 1968.

Karen and Ron work together as Senior Regional Directors in their very large international business which generates sales of more than $9 million per year in Australia and New Zealand. After the Australian parent company bought the world rights for Nutri-Metics International, Karen and Ron expanded their business to the US, Canada, UK, Greece and Hong Kong.

Much time is now spent travelling to these countries to further develop new territories which are showing enormous promise for the future.

Ron and Karen hold an unbeaten world record in the direct selling industry for team sales having sold more than $1 million of Nutri-Metics each year for 18 consecutive years.

Karen believes in teaching people to start their own business using very little capital in order to expand the most important commodity of all - personal development of others. "Many people don't even know they have the skills," Karen says. **"Our philosophy is to help people help other people."**

A former David Jones' house model and Vogue cover girl, Karen finds the opportunity to create her own future and that of others extremely exhilarating as well as challenging. She combines business acumen, discipline, her **unique creativity and entrepreneurial flair to develop her business.** She is dedicated to excellence and professionalism and to this end she keeps up-to-date in the field of cosmetology, skin care and innovative marketing techniques.

Karen's career in fashion and modelling led to radio and television and she became an on-camera personality for a national program for 15 years and Ron and Karen had their own radio program, The Two Of Us, on Brisbane's ABC radio. But both Karen and Ron felt radio, TV and fashion did not give them the lifestyle, family time and economic security they wanted.

A desire for greater financial rewards led them to explore direct selling. Karen had already had experience of Nutri-Metics through her mother, Mrs Rasmus who was the company's first Australian consultant. "My mother has been a continual source of inspiration," Karen says. **"She is a beautiful woman who displays fortitude, compassion and an optimistic spirit through all circumstances."**

Karen and Ron Brady have developed their business together. They can both do everything needed to run the business successfully. "The only thing that Ron does not do are the facials," Karen says. "But he manages the banking, financial administration, organises functions, recruits and trains. We work the business together."

Karen believes women should be recognised for their talents and equally rewarded for their efforts. **"Many women give up too soon.** They don't believe in themselves. They need to learn to cope with rejection and to bounce back and have another go," she says.

Ron and Karen run live-in development and Leadership Seminars both for Senior Directors and their consultants.

Karen's involvement with people allows her interest of fashion and personal presentation to come to the fore. She believes nothing is more important for people in business than proper presentation. **"There's no second chance to gain a first impression," she says.** Karen has been nominated for the International Woman Entrepreneur of the Year to be announced in London at the annual conference for women entrepreneurs.

SANDY'S SUCCESS IN CALIFORNIA

SANDY MCDONALD
NUTRI-METICS

Sandy McDonald from Sydney is a stunningly gorgeous blonde and a dynamic Senior Regional Director with Nutri-Metics. At just 30, she has the world at her fingertips. She has spent the past ten years building her Nutri-Metics business and reached the top level after just four years.

Sandy left school at the end of Year 10 and became a booking agent for a modelling agency. Her initial motivation for starting her own business, was to earn a car. Once she had joined Nutri-Metics, she found tremendous inspiration in the company's CEO, Imelda Roche, and in Roger and Naomi Alberts.

"I loved the product and soon became successful because I was totally dedicated and committed to what I was doing," she says of her meteoric rise. **"I love people and I am very goal oriented. I lead by example and I feel responsible for my team's success.** I give them a sense of belonging."

She says her business has given her the chance to do everything. **She is a wife, a mother and has grown both personally and financially.** "I feel I can tackle anything and I have enormous confidence in myself. Nothing is too overwhelming."

"I have a happy and secure marriage and my husband Ken feels he is part of my success," she says. Sandy believes she would not have achieved all she has without his backing. Ken has joined Sandy's business on a full-time basis. They have allotted themselves different roles according to their strengths. Ken looks after the financial assets, property acquisition, business administration and international development.

Sandy says her business has had a very positive effect on her children. **"They have become very independent and are instilled with the role model of a positive work ethic."**

Sandy and Ken took their Nutri-Metics business to California 18 months ago. She has found exposure to American society very stimulating. "I think they are 20 years ahead. They are very evolved; different things happen in their communities; they talk actively about events and deal with problems by going for counselling."

Sandy has realised they also want **quick returns for their efforts** and has streamlined her training to create faster results for her US recruits. She is now based in Newport Beach and is loving her American business experience.

"I love the American attitude towards success. **Everyone has a dream to get to the top.** In Australia the average person is still apologetic about being ambitious."

She says her ten years with Nutri-Metics has brought her more life experience, excitement and rewards than most people have in a lifetime. **"I adore my business and have a vision for a global network."**

Sandy is a wonderful role model for other young women. Along with financial independence at 30, and a balance between family and business, **she has retained her femininity and embraced success to the full.**

SUCCESS IS GREEK FOR DEANNA

DEANNA AND MICHAEL PURZA
NUTRI-METICS

Adelaide based Deanna Purza is unquestionably one of the most individual and dynamic women to embrace Nutri-Metics as a career.

She was born in Greece and emigrated to Australia when she was eight. She married an Australian and had all but forgotten her birthplace when she was offered an opportunity to help set up Nutri-Metics there.

Her knowledge of Greek emerged from the deep recesses of her mind and within four days of returning, she was able to give a four-hour seminar in her mother tongue. Without waiting for the dust to settle, Deanna wanted to be in on ground floor level. In less than a year in Greece she has two directors and four directors elect.

"I found the women in Greece were very open to embracing the Nutri-Metics opportunity," she says. **"Their eyes would light up and there was amazing energy in the room. It was so refreshing."**

These women were very conscious of their presentation and image. They always took the trouble to look good and wear their best. "I did not find them held back by culture or tradition. If they perceived Nutri-Metics as good for them and their families, they would single-mindedly decide to get involved."

Deanna, 47, likes to look at life through the big picture. "Our emotions are excited by big skies, mountain tops and great personal achievements. **We need to be a player in life - not just a spectator. Nutri-Metics is about action and achievement."**

She joined the company 13 years ago and it took her ten years to become a Senior Regional Director which took her earnings to six figures. Deanna is married and has two children, a son aged 26 and a 16 year old daughter.

Hard work has paid Deanna well. She has developed her **personal skills and a positive mental attitude to both herself and her career.** These were the qualities that enabled her to be a leader. Now others want to emulate her.

"My business has expanded my self esteem and helped enormously with my ability to get on with all kinds of people. Many of my work colleagues have become great friends. **The world has become my oyster with extensive travel and time to share my experience with others,"** she says.

Deanna's goals are to help enrich the lives of others and to share with them the benefits of her own experience. She says she keeps fit and healthy with a mixture of good diet, exercise, sleep and friendship.

"My husband and children have always been supportive. My greatest obstacle has been to deal with periodic self doubt that sometimes overwhelms me." At this time she has drawn upon character and determination to lift herself out of these "pits of despair".

"Success is a journey, not a destination. I believe the journey is the most exciting part, the learning, the growing, the maturing along the way. Most of all it is the fun and the friends."

OLE MEXICO! FOR TRACEY
TRACEY AND LEON WAXMAN
NUTRI-METICS

Nutri-Metics has given Tracey Waxman the chance to experience an international dimension to her life. The beautiful, warm, friendly 32 year old Sydney-based mother, **has pioneered her company's products in Mexico.**

"It has been enormously exciting and challenging," she says. "I've learned to operate in a whole new business environment and to get to know another culture, language and country."

After Tracey had her first child, a daughter who is now six, she decided she did not want to go back to her profession as an occupational therapist in a hospital. "I spent three months doing lunch, playgroups and exercise classes before I felt myself getting restless. I needed new stimulation," she says.

Tracey was introduced to Nutri-Metics six years ago by her mentor and role model, Sandy McDonald. **"For the first year I enjoyed the business as a social director. I had no financial pressure and saw it as a way of working my own hours while still being a mother," she says.**

She now has a son aged two and has turned her business into an extremely rewarding family concern. "At the end of my first year I went to the seminar in Palm Springs, US. Here I first experienced some of the incentives and rewards in the business. My husband, Leon, had been supportive from the beginning. The following year he joined me on the seminar and realised how many men were involved with the business."

After almost five years, Leon decided to join Tracey. "He's helped me develop the international dimension. He has brought to the business his management skills and has been able to counsel women and help them develop their futures."

Tracey has a genuine interest in other people. **"I also like being my own boss, setting my own challenges and my own pace**, and being a leader. As the leader I know I have to be credible and to provide people with ways of finding their own motivation and solutions," she says.

Tracey says she thrives on stress. "I like being really busy and having lots of things happening. **The adrenalin keeps me going.**"

She says her husband's support and encouragement has been the major reason for her success. "He has been able to support me both physically and emotionally. **He believed in me, and my success only enhanced our relationship. He is a very full-on father and both children benefit from both parents working from home or are equally content with either of us on their own.**"

Being able to give women a vehicle to transform themselves has been one of the most satisfying elements of her career. **"I feel Nutri-Metics is a vehicle to empower women with the opportunity to create financial security, independence and personal development. This business is a special gift to offer others."**

LIFE IS WHAT YOU MAKE OF IT

FREDA AND WAYNE LAWRENCE
RAWLEIGH PTY LTD

In the past ten years, Freda and Wayne Lawrence from Wollongong, NSW have established a group that stretches across Australia from Darwin to Hobart, and from Perth to Lord Howe Island. The couple have an annual income of more than $70,000 which they achieved in just three years.

The Lawrence's chose Rawleigh because they liked the product and the 104 year old company had a good reputation. Freda, now 47, continued to work as a registered nurse until 1992. They have four children aged between 12 and 22.

"Because our team is so scattered, it is not possible to meet them all regularly," Freda says. "Our most important role is communication which we do through a monthly newsletter, our 0055 hotline, welcome and congratulatory letters and regular workshops. We also talk regularly on the telephone to our leaders. **Our telephone bills are a delight to Telecom.**"

Wayne and Freda have made many new friends through Rawleigh. **"We also love the flexibility of working time, we like always being at**

home for our family," Freda says. "For me personally, I have developed confidence in my own abilities to mix with my peers and to speak in front of a large audience."

The couple have set many exciting goals for the future. They get so much enjoyment from their work, they don't believe they will ever retire from the business.

"I enjoy the variety of tasks," Freda says. "Because I work fairly long hours, I catnap in the afternoon. An hour lying down does wonders for the mind and the body." She does no regular exercise, but makes sure she walks whenever possible.

"The business has had many positive effects on the children," she says. "They enjoy having both parents at home for most of the day and have come with us on numerous overseas trips. **I believe life is what you make of it.** Everyone has many opportunities offered to them. Some people take advantage of these, others do not. If you do the best you can in life then you have achieved."

Freda sees setbacks as a learning experience. "They are an opportunity to grow as a person. My greatest obstacle was overcoming the negative attitude of some friends and family. When people say, 'that won't work', it sets you thinking whether you are doing the right thing. Oh boy, I'm glad I didn't listen."

WORKING SMARTER NOT HARDER

SUE AND BRIAN UPTON-RICHMOND
LE REVE

Sue Upton-Richmond first began direct sell-ing to earn enough to buy a washing machine and earn a few extra dollars. She has been involved in direct selling, insurance and the per-sonnel industry for 24 years and was part of the team that set up Le Reve three years ago. Today she earns more than $100,000 a year.

In December 1992, Sue and her husband Brian, who is also with Le Reve, became Senior Executive Directors of the company and were presented with two beautiful Mazda sports cars.

"For Brian and I, Le Reve has been a dream come true. My husband has been my greatest inspiration and encouragement," says Sue, who was also the first woman to become national president of SWAP, an organisation for professional sales people.

The aspects that have impressed her most about Le Reve are the com-pany's honesty, integrity and win-win philosophy. "I had reached the top level in another company so I looked very carefully before making the deci-sion to join Le Reve."

Sue believes her success is due to her personal determination. "I also owe it to experience, leadership qualities, ability to visualise what I want and to set goals to achieve it. I believe in working smart not hard."

She says being a leader is more important than being a manager. "Always be prepared to do what you ask your team to do," she says.

Sue has experienced many personal and financial setbacks in life but looks upon each as a learning experience. She has been a diabetic since she was 19 but has not let that interfere with her determination to reach great heights in business.

"My business has given me an enormous amount of personal growth and I have learned to work with others and to understand people."

Sue has learned strategies to help her cope. She deals with problems before they become stressful, has relaxation time on the weekends and enjoys reading to unwind.

Sue has two grown children from her first marriage and a stepdaughter from her second marriage.

The Le Reve plan is clearly superior to any I have seen both from the point of view of a consultant or a woman who is only looking for a way to supplement her income on a part-time basis.

"I love the products. The company has excellent leadership and as this is a young company, there is a groundfloor opportunity."

FROM REAL ESTATE TO REALITY

MARIA AND TED LEE
PRO-MA SYSTEMS

Maria Lee and her husband Ted were running a real estate company on the Gold Coast. They have two children and although they were making good money they realised the **inherent insecurity in their business**. The property market has its peaks and troughs. Besides that they were at the mercy of huge multi-national property developers.

Maria was introduced to Grace cosmetics almost eight years ago. She became a distributor and she worked her business alongside her real estate career. Gradually she began to see some exciting possibilities in the Grace/Pro-Ma systems business in direct selling.

Pro-Ma's founders, Val and Sandra Fittler made her **feel special, important and worthwhile.** She felt the company offered her a future career and a lifestyle for her family which was congruent with her philosophy and beliefs.

Maria believes once she made a commitment she had a positive expectancy about her business. She was willing to work hard and she found it rewarding to see people grow and be successful. "This business also offered me personal growth as well as the opportunity to work as a family unit. **I love the Pro-Ma products**," she says.

She has her own personal daily self-development program. Both Maria and Ted encourage their family to **"treasure map"** together. They set goals, share them and support each other in achieving them. "Children live up to your expectations of them. You need to have character goals for your children not just doing goals," Maria says.

As a family they have fun and laugh together. They love people and have now taken on the challenge of setting up Pro-Ma in Canada. They have received wonderful support from the Fittler family who set up in Calgary in a beautiful new building.

The Lees hope to establish Pro-Ma as the number one company in Canada. They have faith and hope in the future and they believe their company has strong foundations.

VIVACIOUS, FEMININE AND SUCCESSFUL

MARIE AND DAVID WORDEN
ALOETTE

Marie Worden, 36, is a beautiful, vivacious blonde. When she started in Aloette as a consultant nine years ago she was motivated by a need to earn extra grocery money. "I had low self-esteem and no cash to spend on clothes, cosmetics or luxuries."

Marie had left school, where she had not done well, at 16. "I was categorised as someone who was good with kids and who would make a great mother."

She worked for six years in her father's business before marrying and starting a family. "I loved being a wife and a mother but I felt as if I had no identity. **I joined Aloette and I began to have fun. I felt like a human being again,**" she says.

She learned to take control as her business developed around her. "My husband and I bought a franchise. All of a sudden everything was on my shoulders. I had to pay all the bills, make all the sales happen and be responsible for my team."

The business has enabled her and her husband to co-parent their two children. **"I believe a housewife needs to value herself more,"** Marie says. "I am happy to share roles and my husband has been very supportive. He is the wind beneath my wings."

Part of Marie's success has been her ability to put her nurturing and mothering qualities into developing her team. **"I am always there for them. I don't just see them as a money-making machine.** My team are my ambassadors whether they stay with me or not."

Marie says if you are only enjoying two days out of seven, stop what you are doing and find something you enjoy seven days a week. "Never live your life for weekends only," she says.

Although Marie enjoys being a strong and independent business woman, she still likes being taken care of by a strong man. **She resumes a very feminine role outside the business.** "All women need an identity and women can still be excellent in business yet retain their femininity."

CHAPTER 16

INTERVIEWING THE STARS

Jenny Beckinsall, Avroy Shlain

Anneke Stephan, Avroy Shlain

Judy Allanby, Elmon

Chris Boughen, Elmon

Geri Cvitanovich, Herbalife

Margaret Hobbs, One Earth

Maree Wood, Lady Remington

Barb Fishpaw, Lady Remington

Cathie Cordell, Lady Remington

Trish Sheridan, Lady Remington

Beverley Smith, Reliv

Margaret Jones, Nutri-Metics

Fiona Clarke, Nutri-Metics

Gail Ballment, Learner's World

Sherien and John Foley, Pro-Ma Systems

COMPETITIVE SPIRIT
BRINGS SUCCESS

JENNY BECKINSALL
AVROY SHLAIN COSMETICS

Jenny Beckinsall radiates warmth, friendliness and reliability. She is a woman you feel you can trust.

Jenny, who has been with Avroy Shlain since early 1979, has never looked back. "My career with the company began as a sideline to complement what I called my **'keep busy while you stay at home with the baby business'**," she says.

Jenny ran a slimming and leg waxing business from home but soon realised Avroy Shlain was going to take all her time.

Jenny is a go-getter and achiever at the highest level. She remains at the top of her business year after year while at the same time managing her marriage and her three daughters.

She attributes her success to her competitive nature which she calls her 'killer instinct'. "I don't like to fail. I have a team behind me that is loyal and supportive. It is important to me to develop the talent and potential in each person in my group of distributors. I expect nothing but the best from my team."

Jenny's high standards are very noticeable in her training, her customer service and the meetings she holds. **"If you expect them to do well, they will,"** she says.

"Avroy Shlain transformed me from a mouse in to a monster - a nice one." She has gained confidence in herself, leadership and time management skills and thrives on the numerous opportunities to win prizes and to travel overseas which she and her husband have done each year for the past ten years.

Her husband, Chris, is a tremendous support and very proud of her, especially when she brings home a pay cheque that is larger than his. Their three children appreciate the opportunities their mother has given them and are supportive and proud of her. Most of her business in done in the morning so she is free to be with her daughters in the afternoon.

"I live by the motto, 'do unto others as you would have them do unto you'. **It costs nothing to smile at people and to be nice.** You receive so much in return. I want to get better and better at what I do. I want my area to be the greatest."

Jenny has been nominated four times and won Avroy Shlain's Woman of the Year in 1990. She has won group manager of the year twice. With all these achievements behind her, Jenny will no doubt continue to get better and better.

FLOWER BLOOMS IN
ARID DESERT

ANNEKE STEPHAN
AVROY SHLAIN COSMETICS
Age 33

Imagine a desert flower blossoming under the hot sun in barren surrounds and you will have a very apt description of this dynamic woman. Anneke Stephan hails from a very dry region of South Africa where she lives on a farm with her husband and three children.

When newly married, although she had a teaching degree, Anneke worked alongside her husband on the farm where she did the bookwork and helped with other jobs. Like any woman, she wanted to earn her own money and after attending a demonstration and being impressed with the quality of the product, she put her energy into the Avroy Shlain range.

That was more than ten years ago. "**Believing in the product is most important**," she says. "You have to be able to look people in the eye and honestly tell them that it is an excellent product."

Anneke, now 33, achieves through driving determination to overcome the obstacles in her path. Her area is widespread and is made up mostly of small remote towns and farms. She can travel more than 1100kms in one journey.

She says part of her success is attributable to the women in her team. **"There is trust, loyalty and friendship.** I know I can rely on them unconditionally to get the job done."

Anneke brings her group together at her farm where she trains, encourages and motivates them.

In 1991, she won the coveted Avroy Shlain Woman of the Year title. She has achieved an overseas trip with spending money included for herself and her husband every year she has been with Avroy Shlain. She has a new Mercedes among numerous other benefits.

Anneke's secret to success is her organisational ability. She plans her year in advance down to the smallest detail. She even plans her menus at the farm for a month in advance. Then she relaxes, just a little.

Her motto is: **"If you can dream it, you can do it."** She never gives up and puts her heart and soul into accomplishing a project or goal. **She wants to stay at the top, to always be the best she can be** and never to be just an 'ordinary' distributor. With that positive attitude, she will never be just 'ordinary'.

152

JUDY'S TOPS IN TASMANIA

JUDY ALLANBY
ELMON
Age 35

Judy Allanby, is a bundle of positive, vivacious energy. Her infectious enthusiasm, genuine love of and dedication to her job has resulted in her and her team enjoying many successes.

Since starting with Elmon in April 1990, Judy has progressed from consultant to Group Executive Manager managing the Islanders in Tasmania. Tasmania is third top state in the whole of Australia due to Judy's efforts.

To constantly successful, Judy has been **commited to helping others do well**. "My philosophy has always been to help and encourage and the positive results will follow. **I like to work alongside each of my girls** (as she calls them) and to encourage them. I like to recognise their efforts whether great or small. I'm always proud of them," she says.

Judy says the success of a team comes as a result of all members supporting and encouraging each other. **"Success as a team is not an individual thing. It's sharing knowledge, ideas and inspiration with each other,"** Judy says. With this great team spirit, I can see why 'The Islanders' have so many top performers. Judy has promoted out three managers herself.

Judy Allanby is 35, married and has a six year old daughter. After just three years with Elmon, Judy is able to pay the mortgage, the lease on her car and have money left over.

Before joining the business, Judy was a secretary but she longed for the freedom of being able to work her own hours and to control her own business.

"I choose Elmon because **I loved the top quality products**, the owners and the management were very professional and caring. I think I have been successful because I am determined, I actively set goals and I have a very supportive husband."

"YOU DON'T DRIFT
TO THE TOP OF A MOUNTAIN"

CHRIS BOUGHEN
ELMON
Age 43

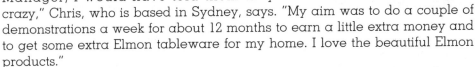

Chris Boughen, 43, who is Sydney based, still feels the same excitement and enthusiasm as she did the day she joined Elmon five years ago.

"If someone could have told me way back in 1988 that today I would be a Group Executive Manager, I would have told them they were crazy," Chris, who is based in Sydney, says. "My aim was to do a couple of demonstrations a week for about 12 months to earn a little extra money and to get some extra Elmon tableware for my home. I love the beautiful Elmon products."

Chris was offered the chance to become a manager after only two months with Elmon. The decision whether she would accept was a difficult one for her as it meant turning her back on a career of 17 years as a teacher.

"But I thought I'd really found my niche in life so I took the plunge and have not regretted it for one minute. Life has changed for me in the past few years. I finally have a passport with stamps from such places as Hawaii, Singapore and New Zealand."

Chris enjoys the people in her Elmon business. **Demonstrations are such fun that I can't really call it working.** My team, The Avengers, is full of enthusiastic and genuinely lovely people. I feel the sky is the limit with Elmon."

Theresa Spence who is the Executive Manager in Australia has had a great influence on Chris's progress through the ranks. "I love the product," says Chris, "and I feel confident of the company and its direction. I love incentives too and I have earned quite a few overseas trips and many household items. My self esteem is much improved."

To cope with stress Chris turns on the answering machine to take time out for herself. She also makes sure her 'vision' remains clear. **"You don't drift to the top of a mountain."**

A MILLIONAIRE IN THE MAKING

GERI CVITANOVICH
HERBALIFE
Age 41

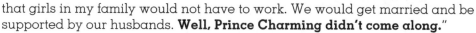

Geri Cvitanovich, 41, was a grocery checker and school teacher in Los Angeles when in answer to an advertisement she walked into the office of Mark Hughes, the founder and director of Herbalife.

"I was miserable," she recalls. "I was desperate to change my situation. I was raised to believe that girls in my family would not have to work. We would get married and be supported by our husbands. **Well, Prince Charming didn't come along.**"

Teaching had seemed like a dependable profession, but despite six years of college education, Geri was not able to earn enough to survive.

"I had to take a second job at the grocery store. I worked in really terrible environments. I was stuck in an inner city school where kids carried guns, knives and were into drugs and gangs. I worked at a sleazy grocery store where people were robbed at gun point all the time. **It was a physically, emotionally and mentally threatening situation.**"

Geri saw Herbalife as her big opportunity to escape to a better life. **It did not need start up capital or sophisticated business experience**. All Mark required of her was that she tried the products first, and if she liked them, to take the products to the market place.

"My first royalty cheque was 97 cents. But that was the biggest milestone of my Herbalife career because to me it was proof that the potential was there."

After 13 years of hard work Geri earns more than $100,000 per month. She says this is due to very good advice from Mark Hughes when she started. **"He said he would groom me to become a millionaire.** He encouraged me to 'do it fast'. He said people will follow you if you are moving. **Treat it like a business from the beginning.**"

Mark told her there were four skills she had to learn: **retailing, sponsoring, training and promoting. He taught her the concept of leverage and he taught her to work smarter, not harder. "Learn to duplicate yourself, that is the key,"** he told her.

At the beginning Geri felt very insecure. **Mark told her to act the part she wanted to be.** He taught her to smile, make eye contact and to have a firm handshake. She practised in front of a mirror with a tape recorder. Mark also told her to **talk to ten people each day about the products and the company**.

Geri had to change her outlook on life. She believed she deserved to make a million dollars and that she could be of value both in the marketplace and to others by giving them financial independence.

"I believe in being around positive people. I also believe people need to keep their dreams alive. They are energized if they live their dreams," she says.

When Geri started her business, she had low self esteem and great insecurity. "I gradually learned the process of accepting responsibility in my business. I now believe we can be anything we want in this lifetime. I have a life filled with joy. **I laugh and love a lot and I share this with others.**"

Her financial independence has given her time to spend with family, **time for personal pampering and great internal growth. Geri is a very inspiring lady.**

BUSINESS IS A FAMILY AFFAIR

MARGARET HOBBS
ONE EARTH (FORMERLY L'AROME)
Age 57

In the three years Margaret Hobbs has been with One Earth, her income has doubled each year.

Although she carries out her business as a regional marketing manager for One Earth part time in conjunction with managing her husband's chiropractic office in Merimbula, NSW four days a week, she has a full time attitude to direct selling.

Her background was in teaching and education. She taught for 11 years and spent 12 years raising her three children and three step children. She has been an office manager for 15 years and established and co-ordinated two community transport services on the NSW south coast for which she has been awarded a special fellowship by the Rotary Club of Merimbula.

Margaret's motivation for becoming involved in the direct selling business was to have regular contact with her children and grandchildren who lived inter-state. **She also wanted the mobility to be able to travel overseas and to have an ongoing income.**

Margaret, now 57, chose One Earth because she was impressed by their products, as well as the caring, helpful attitude of her sponsor and the easy accessibility for everyone to the management team.

"My success has been due to support from One Earth management, my own determination to succeed and my husband's constant encouragement," she says. "I believe as a leader I need to set an example of integrity, trust, enthusiasm and action. **I treat my team as a family, and support and encourage them to achieve goals.**" She also teaches her team how to be independent.

Her business has given her considerable personal satisfaction especially in the area of helping other women improve their self esteem and confidence. She has enjoyed trips to Bali and Hawaii and has a great feeling of achievement in a new field of work that she only started in the "middle of her life".

She copes with stress by analysing problems, trying to modify her own reactions and by not worrying about things beyond her control.

Margaret's goals are to be financially independent, maintain a productive, exciting and healthy lifestyle and to participate in One Earth's expansion in the Asia Pacific region.

Her husband David is a professional person in his own right. He is very proud of her achievements and is totally supportive and encouraging. "My whole family has benefited by the increased opportunities," she says. Four of her children have also joined One Earth.

Margaret's special philosophy is to **'make the most of your talents and take advantage of life's opportunities'**. She and David thrive on challenge and look forward to bigger and better things with their business. **At the time other couples think about retiring and winding down, Margaret and David are poised to enjoy greater challenges and business expansion.**

UNLIMITED INCOME POTENTIAL

MAREE WOOD
LADY REMINGTON FASHION JEWELRY

When Perth-based Maree Wood was made redundant from her job as a window dresser she decided to look for a career that offered something different. **She wanted an opportunity that would allow her to use her talents in new directions.**

She loved fashion and liked the idea of having **unlimited income potential**. When the opportunity came up to join Lady Remington, she knew it was right for her. "It was a new company and I had a ground floor opportunity," she says.

Maree has become successful through her persistence and determination. "I set goals, I love my company and my product and I always strive to do my best," she says.

To be a good leader, Maree believes you must lead from the front and be a good role model. "I have made lots of wonderful friends from my business. **It has also built up my confidence level dramatically**. It has proved to me that when you put your mind to something you can achieve anything you want to. It gives me a great pride to watch people grow."

If she has a problem, Maree talks it over with her husband, Kim or with Elizabeth and Gary Miller who are directors of the company. **To keep fit and relaxed, Maree goes to the gym three times a week and meditates each night before she goes to sleep.**

Maree's husband Kim has been a major part of her success. "He is always giving me encouragement and support. He also helps behind the scenes."

Maree's biggest obstacle was making the final decision to take her life in a different direction. "The business was all new to me. But I believe that **persistence and determination are the keys**. When you have goals and dreams and you really put your mind to something, you can achieve anything you want in life."

LIVING THE AMERICAN DREAM

BARB FISHPAW
LADY REMINGTON FASHION JEWELRY

Barb Fishpaw is a zone vice president for Lady Remington Fashion Jewelry in Lima, Ohio USA. Barb's story is newsworthy in that it fits with today's poor economy and ways to overcome financial despair.

The Fishpaws are examples of living the American dream. They overcame unemployment and jobs with no future. Today they earn a six-figure income and there are more than 150 people working under them.

Barb has done much to implement Lady Remington's training programs and has devised **a successful, creative and fun way to help build the business.** She has been teaching the technique to the whole company through a training video that she has helped develop.

ACCOUNTANT NOW ADDS
BIGGER NUMBERS

CATHIE CORDELL
LADY REMINGTON FASHION JEWELRY

Cathie Cordell of Chambersburg, Pennsylvania, USA has been in the direct selling industry since she was 14 years old. Now, 27 years later, she is a zone vice president with Lady Remington and is running her business full time from home.

In the past, Cathie used direct selling as a way to supplement her salary as a government accountant. She got tired of not being her own boss and not having flexibility at work - especially when her children were sick.

At that point she decided to make direct selling a full-time career and supplement her husband's salary.

"Lady Remington has taught me valuable leadership skills and allows me to meet new people. **I love the product and the service Lady Remington gives to its sales representatives and consumers,**" she says.

Cathie has 300 people working under her and is generating a handsome income.

PART-TIME JOB LEADS TO
THE BIG TIME

TRISH SHERIDAN
LADY REMINGTON FASHION JEWELRY

Trish Sheridan has been in direct selling for 14 years, five and a half of which have been with Lady Remington. At 21, she started in direct selling to fill her spare time. Trish worked full-time in an accounting position and was in direct selling part-time.

When she had children, she quit her job to pursue direct selling as a full-time career which she ran from home in New Jersey.

Trish has been Lady Remington's **number one seller for more than five months** in 1992 and 1993. She has 50 people working under her.

"Lady Remington has built my self-confidence and I have no problem speaking to big groups of people. With direct selling I have surpassed my income from my accounting job and I am an equal contributor to my household."

The Sheridans are now renovating their home - all paid for in cash from Lady Remington earnings.

Trish and her family love all the perks her business offers, especially the free travel earned for outstanding achievement.

A PERFECT VEHICLE TO WEALTH AND HEALTH

BEVERLEY SMITH
RELIV
Age 53

In less than two years after joining Reliv, Beverley Smith is earning $18,000 per month. The charming 53 year old who lives in Sydney has a network of thousands and feels so good she is training for a triathlon (10 km running, 20 km cycling and 1 km swimming).

Bev was a trained nurse who had spent some time in the party plan business and later with a personal growth academy. At the time Reliv came into her life, Bev and her partner had retired and set off on a yacht. The boat developed engine trouble and when they stopped to have it repaired, friends invited them to a Reliv party.

"I started to take the product and discovered my energy had increased," Bev says. "I felt healthier and had a greater sense of well-being."

Her first commission cheque paid for the repairs to the boat and she became inspired by the business. **"I wanted to help others achieve both health and wealth.** I began to get constant calls from people who said how great they felt."

The mother of three children aged 28, 29 and 30, has been inspired by Reliv's founder, Dr Koligris who believes people do not need to get degenerative diseases. The formula he devised is claimed to vastly improve the health of people on his program.

Reliv has certainly improved Bev's life. Her business has grown quickly and she aims to get her friends to the same level she has reached. "The company has an excellent infrastructure and I have organised telephone conference calls to make communication with my network easier."

Bev has come from a background of helping people and has now found the **perfect vehicle to create both health and wealth. She is a gentle, caring person which is a far cry from the usual image of a pressurised sales person.**

EXTRAORDINARY LIFE FOR ORDINARY PEOPLE

MARGARET JONES
NUTRI-METICS

Margaret Jones who is based in Auckland was one of the first Nutri-Metics consultants in New Zealand when she joined in 1972. With two sons aged five and three, she wanted to supplement the family income without disrupting her children's upbringing.

Her husband got behind her and together they built a thriving team. Through sales in their first year they achieved first level of directorship, international seminars in Los Angeles and Mexico and a company car.

"Nutri-Metics provided an income and a lifestyle with the benefits of being able to advance our personal growth and development," Margaret says. "It allowed me to be the manager of my own business with flexible hours, to learn people skills and to become adept in the organisation and training of successful personnel."

In 1974, Margaret's sales success won her family a trip to Fiji. She also reached Regional Directorship and a new Ford Fairlane car that year. She built up a team of more than 200 consultants and directors.

In the late '70s her marriage broke down and she relinquished Regional Director status and returned to consultant level. "It was certainly hard to do but as I look back, it was the best move at the time. I had to concentrate on the emotional and personal side of my life."

She rebuilt the business and in 1984 was again a Regional Director. In the past eight years she has built up a team of more than 600 consultants. In 1991, she received a million dollar award trophy for reaching with her team more than $1 million sales during a year.

She bought a home and paid it off in just nine years which is a remark-able achievement for a single mother. Her company replaces her Honda Accord every two years and she travels overseas twice a year.

"Nutri-Metics offers an extraordinary lifestyle for ordinary people who are prepared to work," Margaret says. "My future looks bright. I have finan-cial independence, self development, more travel, the cars and the prospect of managerial advancement - and all from a job I thoroughly enjoy."

BALANCING BABIES, BUSINESS AND BRENT

FIONA CLARKE
NUTRI-METICS
Age 29

Fiona Clarke, 29, has been with Nutri-Metics in Wellington, New Zealand, for five and a half years. Within six months of joining the company, she was able to leave her job as a primary school teacher to pursue her new career full-time. She has since had two children, Jessica who is now three and Mathew, who is one.

Fiona's motivation for joining Nutri-Metics was the **challenge of selling as well as the chance to work part time**. She wanted the freedom to choose her own activity level.

Initially her husband, Brent, didn't believe she would be a success. Now he has learned to cope with the change of lifestyle the business demands. For example the numerous phone calls during the evening, people coming and going and the evenings when she must be out.

On the other hand, he has enjoyed the positive side to Fiona's success which includes the car, the trips and the income. "Brent has gradually adjusted to the change and the work ethic necessary to make the business a success." **Fiona says her challenge is to balance family life with a career. "I'm still working on it."**

Fiona has been inspired by her Senior Regional Director, Maureen Wagg, who has taught her about leadership. Fiona believes in leading by example and having a caring business relationship with her team.

"My own self confidence has developed enormously," she says. "I am a more accomplished public speaker and I have developed **a personal image that I am happy with. I feel more decisive and confident in my ability to assert myself."**

NUMBER ONE IN TOYS SALES

GAIL BALLMENT
LEARNER'S WORLD
Age 38

Gail Ballment is 38 years old and has been with Learner's World for more than ten years. She operates out of Brisbane in Queensland and from the day she joined she has been the highest paid consultant in the company. Gail left school after Year 10 and become a receptionist. She was married at 20 and now has three sons. Her reasons for joining the business were the desire to have flexible hours, to be her own boss and to be able to write her own pay cheques.

Gail was also attracted to the company in the hope that she could help her children with their education and provide the same service for other parents.

Gail's success has been due to her hard work, determination and persistence. "I lead by example and provide good support for my team. I always maintain a positive attitude and I am able to relate well to my demonstrators."

Her aim is to develop her training skills even further and to remain the number one directorate in Australia. "My husband has been very supportive and has offered me a lot of encouragement. **My greatest challenge has been to manage my home, children and business while my husband is away.**"

HOLD ONTO THE BIG PICTURE

SHERIEN AND JOHN FOLEY
PRO-MA SYSTEMS

Sherien and John Foley started in the Pro-Ma business when it first began in 1983. John was in the legal profession and Sherien was an actress with her own television show. They were not looking for anything. Then John met Val Fittler.

"Val had a vision," he says. "He said he was going to build Pro-Ma into the largest marketing company in Australia and was going to take Pro-Ma into every country in the world. I looked at Val and thought to myself, "you little so-and-so, you might just do it", and told him I was in. I wanted to be part of this vision."

CHAPTER 17

WINNING WOMEN

Barb Thoms, Mary Kay

Norelle Turner Allen, Mary Kay

Ester Porta, Mary Kay

Lynn Duncan, Mary Kay

Kris Behan, Nu Skin

Dene Johnson, Nu Skin

Chris Longfelder, Nu Skin

Maria Douglas, Undercover Underwear

Marie Ferrell, Undercover Underwear

Merle Anderson, World Book

Philomena Masters, World Book

Marcia Griffin, Pola Cosmetics

THERE'S A MAN IN MY KITCHEN

BARB THOMS
MARY KAY
Age 38

Barb Thoms, 38, is an elegant, well-groomed lady. She has been with Mary Kay for more than 11 years and is now an executive senior director with a Perth-based team of consultants.

Barb was a secretary before her sons, now aged seven and 11, were born. After being retrenched from what she describes as her 'proper job', she felt bitter and as though someone else had control over her destiny.

She joined Mary Kay so she could develop a business in which she had control over her life. The main attraction for her was **a balanced lifestyle** where she could enjoy success in her personal and business life. Her role model was Michele Giderson who as top national sales director at Mary Kay made the job look easy.

Barb's determination and her fierce competitive spirit have contributed towards her success. **She is always competing against her own best result and continually sets herself new and exciting challenges.** She has set her sights on reaching the top and does not waiver from that goal. Barb believes that to be a successful leader she must lead by example; show rather than tell and build a belief in her team that they too can reach their goals.

Barb says her business has gone a long way towards achieving all that she hoped it would. **She now has more confidence, and the strength to reach the heights she had always felt she was capable of reaching.** At the same time her stress level has been greatly reduced.

"I find gardening relaxing and therapeutic. I believe I am a calm and even tempered person who is consistent in my moods and my approach," she says. **"I feel that what you give out will come back to you. If you do the right thing, good things will happen."**

Barb Thoms's greatest challenge has been the process of accepting that some people will leave the business. "People's lives change and they make choices. I don't see anything as an obstacle and I don't doubt my own ability."

In the beginning, Barb's husband was negative about her business. But it made her more determined to prove it could work. **Now he is very supportive.** "He had to see the tangible benefits first," she says. "Now he has left his job and we have reversed roles. He has become the homemaker. **He cooks, shops, takes care of the children and smoothes the way so everything I do can be done easily.** He has enough confidence in himself to handle this situation. He is not threatened."

Barb and her husband have goals in common and work closely together. I'm sure this scenario is every woman's dream.

PERSISTENCE PAYS OFF

NORELLE TURNER ALLEN
MARY KAY
Age 39

Norelle Turner Allen, who is Brisbane-based, has been with Mary Kay for more than 17 years. She is now 39 and was a trained nurse before she started her full-time business. She has three teenage children who were the motivation for starting her own business. She wanted to be able to work around their needs.

Norelle joined Mary Kay because she loved the products and was inspired by the founder of the business, Mary Kay Ash. Norelle has reached the level of Executive Director.

"I believe in being persistent, in having a goal and in leading by example," Norelle says. "My business success has brought me enormous personal growth, increased self esteem and emotional independence."

To cope with stress, Norelle walks every day. She also enjoys cooking and reading. "I live my life by the philosophy that you get back what you put in and it is better to give than to receive. As for my lifestyle, I now know that rather than just existing, Mary Kay has given me the chance to give my children a private school education and already I am seeing the benefits of that investment.

"It has also given my husband the opportunity in times of recession to change vocation and begin a new business, without worrying about our financial commitments to day to day living. **My career with Mary Kay allows me to drive a top of the range Fairlane instead of numerous second hand cars. In fact pink cars have been a way of life for more than 14 years."**

Norelle has travelled extensively overseas. Before Mary Kay she had never been outside Queensland. "One of the highlights would certainly be taking our three children to America and Disneyland. To see the delight on their faces certainly made my goal complete."

MARY KAY PUTS LYNN IN THE PINK

LYNN DUNCAN
MARY KAY NZ
Age 46

Lynn Duncan, 46, married a New Zealand barrister and moved from Canada where she had worked as a production expeditor in a factory. She wore a hard-hat and steel-capped shoes. It is a long way from the glamorous cosmetics world in which she now works.

She had already used Mary Kay products for 12 years in Canada and she wasn't moving to New Zealand without two year's supply. Lynn found out that Mary Kay Cosmetics was arriving as she did and she became a pioneer consultant. Mary Kay Ash, founder of Mary Kay, was her inspiration and role model. She has been with the business for five years and is senior sales director. It took her only six months to reach this level and she now earns more than $6,000 a month. **She drives the only pink Ford Fairmont in New Zealand.**

Lynn, who lives in Auckland, is highly organised and has a very professional attitude towards her business. She loves to be busy and enjoys travelling. In Canada she had been a political candidate for three elections.

Now she is getting the career satisfaction she needs from Mary Kay. "I love the flexibility. **I control my own life and I feel highly motivated by that.**" Lynn likes to lead by example. "I don't ask people to do what I wouldn't do. I'm dynamic and I get things done. I like to talk about problems as they come up. I help others to be as successful as they want to be. I find it difficult to deal with people who don't have honesty as a principle and with people who feel they are threatened by me."

She says her business has been very challenging. "I was starting a new business and I was starting a new relationship at the same time. **My husband understands how I love my business and how much fun I have.** We discuss how we feel and understand each other's needs."

To cope with stress Lynn has built a beach house to get away. She enjoys warking in the garden to relax. Lynn likes dealing with problems as they come up.

Lynn has a team of 300 women and her annual sales in New Zealand for many products is over $450,000.

Lynn has been a vital link in Mary Kay's success in New Zealand.

167

ESTER AIMS FOR INTERNATIONAL TEAM

**ESTER PORTA
MARY KAY
Age 48**

Eighteen years ago, Ester Porta, 48, **emigrated to Australia from Argentina**. She had lived in Mendoza where she had a beautiful home and held a highly respected position dealing with environmental issues for the government.

But with the political uncertainty in Argentina during the 1970s, the country became violent, insecure and unsettled. "I felt I needed to move my family to safety and I made a very quick move. **I arrived in Australia with few material assets besides suitcases of clothes.**"

When Ester and her family were placed in an absorption centre on the outskirts of Sydney's western suburbs, they went into a state of culture shock. **"We could not speak a word of English,"** she says. "Within days of arriving my son fell and broke a leg. At the hospital I felt helpless and hopeless when I could not explain to staff what had happened. I decided to learn English - and fast."

After trying over and over and failing to get a job she became disheartened. "My self esteem and confidence began to wane. Then my English tutor advised me to answer yes when I was asked if I spoke English and yes if they asked if I had an previous experience in the position I was applying for." She soon got a job working in a factory.

To brighten their dismal accommodation at the absorption centre, Ester plastered the walls with bright happy faces cut from magazines. **She believed the only way to survive was to look forward**, to believe in a better future and to forget the past. It was over.

She learned English and changed jobs until she became a supervisor in a plastics factory. About that time her marriage came apart, but she was able to buy a home and support her two children on her salary. Her job earned her responsibility and with it, stress. She worked in a very male dominated environment.

She encountered the Mary Kay organisation, but did not realise it was such an opportunity until her circumstances changed once again. She remarried and unexpectedly had a third child. She also fell and hurt her back. The pain made it impossible for her to keep her high pressure job as superintendent so she left and joined her husband in business.

When that went under Ester made another career change. She became a mediator and counsellor for the Smith Family. Through this she spoke to hundreds of single mothers who could not, or did not seem to have the will to support their families.

"I became depressed so I contacted Mary Kay again and said: 'I'm determined. What can I do to earn a pink Fairlane car?'." **Within six months she had become a director and earned her car**. At the time she was the second woman to achieve this is such a short time. She is working for a round the world trip.

"Now I have a mission. **I want to help other women develop their potential. I want to have a successful woman in my team from every nationality and I want to help others to believe in themselves. Never give up your dream.**"

FROM HOUSEWIFE TO INTERNATIONAL BUSINESSWOMAN

KRIS BEHAN
NU SKIN
Age early 40s

Kris Behan was born in Texas to a traditional family. **She believed she was destined to marry and become a housewife.** She married a Mexican businessman.

Her first husband was very chauvinistic. "He was an extremely successful businessman but he saw no need to share or discuss his financial dealings with me," she says. "I felt the need to understand our family finances and took a course in taxes. **For the first time I went out of my comfort zone into what I had considered a males-only domain.**"

She found it easy to understand the whole financial picture and stopped seeing herself as a "dizzy, empty-headed housewife". "All of a sudden the lights went on in my head. My mind had begun to work."

Kris also took a real estate course and began to feel she was breaking free from a prison of ignorance. "My husband was very threatened by my emerging knowledge and I realised I had been going through the motions of life while remaining numb inside. The relationship was dead." She made a decision to break free. Her father loaned her the money for a divorce lawyer and she began a new life.

Kris met up with Tom whom she had dated at college 20 years earlier. "He had the qualities I was looking for. **He had a strong sense of self, he was prepared to treat me on an equal basis and most of all, we had a lot of fun.**"

Kris joined Tom in Alaska. It was there she was introduced to Nu Skin. She wanted to start her own business but did not have the capital. **Nu Skin appealed to her because of its low start up cost and because she could operate from her living room.**

Kris qualified as an executive on her own and her second husband, Tom who is in the health and fitness business, has become interested in the nutritional aspects of the Nu Skin product line.

Nu Skin has given Kris and Tom an international lifestyle, the opportunity to travel and to share new and exciting experiences together.

BLUE DIAMOND IN THE MAKING

DENE JOHNSON
NU SKIN

Dene Johnson who lives in San Francisco, US, is an extremely attractive woman in her late 30s. She is the mother of two sons aged six and seven and has been with Nu Skin for almost three years.

Dene had spent many years in corporate life in the pharmaceutical business. When her husband got transferred, she had to leave her position and all that she had built up and developed was lost. She had to start again in a new territory and in a new area. She had confidence and had already learned the value of persistence.

Dene was attracted to Nu Skin by the idea that whatever she put in would be hers. She also had seen her friends, Russ and Linda Carlen, Nu Skin Blue Diamonds, climb the company's ladder. As their pay cheques became more impressive, Dene was forced to take a more serious look at their business. "At first I was both skeptical and negative," she says. "Then I decided to give it a go on a part time basis."

In her first 14 months, Dene says she learned more than she had in 11 years of previous business experience. **She was rewarded with great personal growth and developed an even greater self confidence, particularly in public speaking.**

Dene's ambition is to become a Blue Diamond and to take Nu Skin to 44 countries. She would also like to travel and do business. **"I believe if you want something badly enough, you can do it,"** she says.

FINANCIALLY DRIVEN FUN

CHRIS LONGFELDER
NU SKIN SEATTLE
Age 42

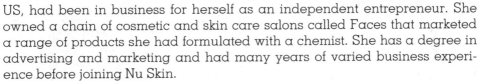

Chris Longfelder's philosophy is "go for it and whatever you do, **have fun along the way**".

Chris, 42, discovered Nu Skin in the spring of 1990. She became an executive in four months and reached 'ruby' status within a year. Her motivation was financial.

Chris who is from Seattle, Washington in the US, had been in business for herself as an independent entrepreneur. She owned a chain of cosmetic and skin care salons called Faces that marketed a range of products she had formulated with a chemist. She has a degree in advertising and marketing and had many years of varied business experience before joining Nu Skin.

"I was immediately attracted to Nu Skin by the concept of **time leveraging, lifestyle benefits and freedom, as well as the abundant income and the ability to start without a huge capital outlay**," she says.

Russ Carlen, her Blue Diamond executive who was instrumental in getting her involved, became her mentor. Chris already had substantial knowledge of skin care products through her own cosmetic business. She was very impressed with the quality of the Nu Skin products.

The factors that contributed to her success were her sales ability, her leadership skills, creativity, determination and the ability to support others. "As a leader, I believe in the need to support my team and follow through on commitments. **I help others to get what they want and not what I want for them**."

Chris says her business has taught her a lot about human nature and how people are motivated. "I now have a greater belief in myself and my own abilities. My future goal is to make more than my husband who is one of the top lawyers in Washington state.

"I discuss my business with my husband and get rid of stress through running. I don't keep any feelings inside." Chris's husband Larry is totally supportive. She says he would love her to be more successful than he is. "He is a great speaker and helps me with my meetings."

Chris has had to cope with people letting her down and not following through when they have signed up. She held steadfast in her vision and confidence in the products after Nu Skin went through considerable media scrutiny in 1991. Her business has prospered.

"**You have to overcome the 'stigma' of network marketing and the bad experiences certain people have had with other companies.** Nu Skin is **very** up front and I believe I have an abundant and exciting future with the company."

Chris is enthusiastic, creative and motivated and has brought a rich range of talents to her business.

MARIA DISCOVERS FORTUNE IN UNDERWEAR

MARIA DOUGLAS
UNDERCOVER UNDERWEAR
Age 52

After being a full-time mother for 16 years, Maria Douglas, 52, decided she needed some mental stimulation. She wanted work that would enable her to still be at home in Brisbane for her three kids, both before and after school.

She had reached Year 8 at school and was a window dresser before she married. Ten years ago she joined Undercover Wear and has been a full-time unit manager since 1986.

Founder and director of the company, Kathy Hood has been Maria's role model. "I chose the company," Maria says, "because it was fully Australian owned and because it donates a percentage of total sales to the Australian Cancer Council."

Maria has always shown willingness to better herself, to work hard and to set goals. As a leader, she believes in showing the way. "I give my team direction. I also appreciate and acknowledge their efforts and try to maintain a good team spirit."

Maria enjoys walking which she says gives her free thinking time. She also loves reading.

At first her husband found it hard when she started her business. He has since grown to become proud of her and her achievements.

Although she had to cope with a serious cancer operation 17 years ago, she has bounced back to a happy and positive attitude. "My greatest obstacle used to be that I had no confidence in myself. I was the little lady who sat in a corner and hoped to goodness no-one would come and talk to me. **That was my greatest fear. Having faced my fear and overcome it, I now know there is nothing in life to fear."**

PARTY PARTY PARTY FOR GRANNY MARIE

MARIE FERRELL
UNDERCOVER UNDERWEAR
Age 53

Marie Ferrell, 53, has been with Undercover Underwear for six years. "**I was an ordinary Aussie battler.** I brought up four children on minimal wages and now I earn more than I ever thought possible!"

Marie has been successful from the word go. "Financially it is getting better every year. Before I joined the direct selling business, I ran the packing department of a kiddies clothing company for 14 years." Marie left school when she was 15 and has been married for 35 years. She has ten grandchildren aged from 14 down to four years.

"I started the business because my husband was on a permanent afternoon shift. I was looking for something to do with my evenings. I did not want to be sitting on my own for a whole lot of years," she says.

Marie was encouraged and taught by Patti Haniford, the NSW state manager. "**My call to Patti was the single best telephone call I have ever made**," Marie says. "I answered an advertisement in a local paper. I didn't know anything about party plan and I was stunned to find I had a real killer instinct when it came to competing. I went for it with a vengeance."

Marie says she has made many new friends and met a lot of 'characters'. "**I really enjoy the competition between teams and I certainly enjoy the money.** My self confidence has grown enormously and I can stand up and speak to a room full of people. If you had asked me to do that six years ago, I would have said you were crazy."

Marie's aim is to ensure she is financially secure for life. After four years of resistance, her husband is now her partner in the business. "**My greatest obstacle was myself. I had not had any dealings with party plan so I am still amazed at the heights that can be reached by hard work and determination.** Nobody is more stunned than me at the achievement of a granny who did not go to parties or give them."

Marie is a great example of age being no barrier to success.

WORLD BOOK WIZARD

MERLE ANDERSON
WORLD BOOK
Age 52

Merle Anderson has been with World Book for more than 27 years. Although both she and her husband were school teachers, Merle discovered she could make more money one or two afternoons a week selling World Book than her husband earned working five full days as a teacher.

Merle was also motivated by the pleasure of independence in business. "Now I am motivated by my love of and belief in our products and I enjoy being part of the huge World Book family."

Merle developed the business while her children were young. She travelled extensively around Australia and started an organisation in almost every town and city in Queensland, northern NSW and rural Victoria.

Merle's great leadership skills have created her success. She believes in rewarding her team with gifts and recognition. **"Never be too busy to drop a one-line cheery message to as many people as you can as often as you can**. Let them know you're thinking of them for whatever reason. Do for your people what other companies would never dream of doing," she says.

Merle's business has given her the chance to travel to about half of the countries of the world. She has developed many skills including public speaking, training, and business development. **"I also have World Book friends in most towns in Australia."**

Merle has developed a constructive way of dealing with crises. "I take stock of where I'm at. I forget temporarily what is not immediately necessary. **I concentrate only on the absolutely urgent**. When the crisis is past I look to planning to ensure the same situation does not arise again."

Merle's husband Alan is fully supportive of her business and he now also works with World Books in a professional corporate role.

Merle's philosophy towards life can be summed up in the following: **"Do unto others as you would have them do unto you - and they will."**

INSPIRATION FROM THE WEST

PHILOMENA MASTERS
WORLD BOOK (AUSTRALIA) PTY LTD

English-born Philomena Masters left school at 15, married at 17 and had a child a year later.

With her newborn baby, and desperately short of money, Philomena had to find a job. She remembers pushing her baby in a pram for eight kilometres each way to get piece work making oxygen masks. She worked on a farm too, to make sure she could have her children with her while she worked.

In 1973 she emigrated to Australia. Although she tried to get work, it was some time before she found a job as a cleaner in a hotel. She stayed there for more than two years until in 1977, someone came to her door selling family encyclopaedia.

"I would have loved to have bought a set of World Books for my daughter. I had to refuse as I didn't have the money," she recalls.

A few moments later the same salesman returned. He offered Philomena the opportunity to earn enough to get her own set of World Books by selling encyclopaedia herself. She began training and felt she was the dunce of the class.

"My self esteem was low. The first time I went to see a client I burst into tears at the front door. Fortunately she was an understanding customer who sat me down and made me a cup of tea and gave me the opportunity to do a presentation.'

Some 14 years later in 1991 Philomena was promoted to state manager for Western Australia. In 1993 she was appointed licensee and has formed her own company that is licenced to sell World Book products. She has a team of more than 360 sales people selling more than $4 million of World Book products per year.

"I haven't tried to invent any new systems. I've done exactly as the company recommends," she says. **"I have built rapport with the customers, established their needs and demonstrated how I could fulfill those needs."**

What she has developed is a way of increasing the amount of sales she achieves from her demonstrations. She did this by increasing the number of closing questions in each demonstration from three to six. She improved her results immediately.

She believes her consistency helped her to be promoted quickly. "I try to never criticise my team, **I lead by example and I have helped others to get what they want**. I learned that my success lies in training others. It has been exciting to see someone grow and develop."

Philomena says she has achieved heights she had never thought of. "I sold 100 sets (of World Books) in ten days in a three-week contest. I got a thrill to see others achieve too. I get very target oriented. **I set a target and I go for it no matter what the obstacles.**"

She believes in treating people the way she wants to be treated. She holds regular meetings and she delegates segments so she can develop others as trainers.

Philomena Masters is a warm, caring and very inspiring woman who has achieved through understanding the process of sharing the opportunity with others.

JET SET TO DIRECT SELLING

MARCIA GRIFFIN
POLA COSMETICS

She had it all. Degrees. A jet-set career. Marriage to a great guy. Then she went into direct selling. "I've never been happier," says Marcia Griffin.

In June 1982 Marcia Griffin turned her back on her career as a top economic adviser for the Wool Corporation and became a Pola consultant — selling cosmetics from a case.

Pola was unknown in Australia. She was its first and only consultant. Today Marcia Griffin is general manager of Pola Cosmetics Australia. The company has almost 3,000 consultants and aims to have 3,400 by the end of 1992.

Pola is a Japanese company founded in 1929. Today it is the world's second biggest direct selling skin care and cosmetic company and has 200,000 consultants world-wide. Marcia Griffin is one of Australia's most successful women. In a recession her company is increasing its sales team. Pola sales are booming.

It's been a personal triumph for Marcia Griffin, who didn't listen when friends begged her not to walk away from a glamorous career.

But she says she gets her greatest satisfaction from seeing women gain the confidence and the self-esteem that comes with the income they earn as Pola consultants. "It's been an experience that's taught me much about women and their place in society."

Marcia believes money is the key to women's independence and that all women should know how to handle finances and control their own income. "Feminists talk about getting equality. When you get financial independence you get equality," she says.

CHAPTER 18

DIRECT SELLING, THE LIFESTYLE OF THE FUTURE

What Does Success Mean

Shared Visions

Is Direct Selling for You?

Dealing with Depression

If Life Deals You Lemons, Make Lemonade

Having a Love Affair with Life

WHAT DOES SUCCESS MEAN

Success for me is doing every day what I want to do." Fabian Dattner. The women I interviewed for this book shared the journey from being dependent and having a low sense of self-esteem to independence and reclaiming a strong sense of self. Many moved from situations of low income and even poverty to financial security and wealth. All of the women derived great benefits from the synergy of working with other women in supportive networks. This social structure acts as an extended family and provides a framework of love and caring.

SUCCESS MEANS

* Starting to feel you are in control of your life.
* Setting targets and knowing you can achieve your goals.
* Being able to cope with change.
* Feeling fulfilled as a women in whichever roles you choose to express your femininity.
* The ability to turn obstacles into opportunity.
* The ability to reframe events and use every experience to your advantage.
* The ability to let go of the past, live in the present and plan for the future.
* The excitement of growing, developing and building a challenging business.
* The joy of expressing your talents and gifts in your life.
* Being able to share your joy in life with people that matter.
* Being able to love yourself.
* Being true to yourself.

IS DIRECT SELLING FOR YOU?

Not everybody has the temperament, personality or desire to get into the business of direct selling. I do not think for one moment that every teacher, nurse, secretary or other professional woman should drop her vocation and start selling cosmetics or nutritional products or soap powder. Your decision to join a direct selling company should be based on a number of factors or a combination of these:

- Would it suit your personality to work alone?
- Can you motivate yourself?
- Do you have the self-discipline to set your own schedule?
- Are you prepared to make the commitment?
- Does it suit your personal needs?
- Do you love the product yourself?
- Are you prepared to use it?
- Are you prepared to recommend it?
- Do you care about other people?
- Do you like other people?

SHARED VISIONS

I am fascinated by those who reach the top because each woman does it in her own special way. All those I interviewed achieved their goal by their own effort, hard work and struggles. What really unites them is a common vision of themselves and the world.

These women all place a great deal of importance on being **optimistic and positive**. They are **proactive** and take responsibility for their lives. They all began with a vision and **the desire and determination** to turn that dream into reality. Every one of them worked very hard and was prepared to discipline themselves by being involved in purposeful activity. They started small and worked themselves up. They were open to learning new skills on the way.

They **reframe their setbacks** and see them as learning experiences. They don't waste time on things they can do nothing about. They let go of the past and move on to the future. They don't dwell in negativity or on past hurts. They do not blame other people for their mistakes. They are prepared to **take advantage of opportunities**. They are **risk takers** and not afraid of new challenges.

They are prepared to **change**. They see their lives as having choices. Many of them have succeeded not because they are ultra-talented or super-woman but because they **persisted**.

They **believe in themselves**. They have to trust their own instincts. They develop the ability to make decisions and have the courage to **use their gifts** and their talents.

Each one of the women I interviewed highlighted her **increased self-esteem** as her major achievement.

Shelley Taylor-Smith world champion long distance swimmer believes she has the ability to redirect pain using her energy. "I filter it through my body. I use it as a positive force not a negative," she says.

Shelley believes there is nothing mystical about success. "You have to know where you're going and what you want. You need to be **focussed and single-minded**. You have to work hard and give 100 per cent of what you've got to give. The drive comes from within and you've got to want to make it happen."

Nutri-Metics chief, Imelda Roche says the direct selling business can be a lonely experience. **"You are working essentially on your own and you need to be self-motivated,"** she says. "You need to have a little more courage, a little more inspiration and a little more discipline to make a success in this industry."

Imelda says motivation comes from within. "It is easy to be lazy, to procrastinate and to look for excuses not to do things. **It takes a strong need and a strong desire to achieve.** It also takes someone with a healthy self-image and a well developed sense of self."

Imelda has four positive, confident children. She believes children of people in Nutri-Metics are exposed to more situations, have more positive input and are encouraged to be involved in the business from an early age.

As Albert Schweitzer said: **"Children learn by three things, example, example, example."** The example of a successful, fulfilled mother is of more value to them than a resentful bored woman, Imelda says.

She encourages women to **get paid help** as soon as they earn sufficient in their directing selling business. "Instead of feeling guilty women should free themselves of domestic drudgery and pay someone else who needs the money and the job."

Imelda says a woman reflects the personality of her family. "If she is happy, fulfilled and relaxed the positive benefits are enormous. It is her responsibility to make herself happy rather than be selfless."

Successful businessperson, Debbie Fields says there are no limitations other than those we impose upon ourselves. "You don't have to be super-mum – or super human to do what you believe in. **Don't be afraid of failing.** The greatest failure is not to try. **'No'** is an unattractive and unacceptable answer. Turn every 'no' into a **'yes'**. **Do what you love to do and the money will follow.** Don't go into the business for money alone. Do it because you love to do it."

IF YOU HAVE TO WALK ON THIN ICE, YOU MAY AS WELL DANCE

There are no guarantees if you go into direct selling you will be successful. You have however very little risk other than a small start up cost, your time and your energy. This is not a get rich quick scheme. Like any business, it takes consistent time and effort.

Many of us have preconceived ideas about the concept of selling. In fact we are all selling ourselves at some level no matter what our business, service or careers.

If you go into this industry you do need to work hard, you do need to be **motivated from within** and you do need to feel **enthusiastic**, about your products. You also need to be able to identify with the philosophy of the company you join, the product and the people with whom you will work.

The upside of this industry is that you will be a changed person through your involvement. Unlike an ordinary job where you do your work and are paid a wage at the end of the week, direct selling is a holistic way of life. The work embraces not only a means to profit, but a career, **a lifestyle and a whole new philosophy of life**.

You will experience the benefit of **support, positive recognition** and reinforcement. There will be leaders wanting you to succeed as much as you do yourself. The benefits of your business success will spill over into your relationships. The opportunity has **no glass ceiling**. There will be no limitations on your promotion or advancement other than those you impose upon yourself.

Salary increases will no longer be an issue, prejudice against promoting women falls away and child care stops being such a critical issue when you are working from home.

DEALING WITH DEPRESSION

Every one of us goes through periods when life seems difficult and we feel down. When I started working on this chapter I stared at the word "depression" and I felt immune. I didn't know what it felt like. It was such a long time since I felt depressed. A few days later, battling a bout of flu, an irate ex-husband and the frustration of not accomplishing my work, I suddenly found myself in that emotional state we call "depressed". I woke in the early hours of the morning feeling anxious and insecure, I lost my usual bouncy sense of confidence, my energy level dropped and I felt tearful and vulnerable.

Women are especially prone to this syndrome and negative feelings which embrace the area of depression. No-one is immune to the emotion. It might be caused by a dramatic life event, such as death, divorce, illness or financial catastrophe. Often it is the accumulation of continuous stress.

We need to know how to cope with periods of depression and how to get ourselves out of the syndrome. I am not talking about either chronic depression or manic depression where professional treatment is needed. I am talking about those down feelings we all experience from time to time.

WHAT WORKS FOR ME

* Having something to look forward to like lunch with a friend.
* Giving myself a treat – a massage, hairdo, aroma therapy.
* Buying something special.
* Going to a great movie.
* Buying an inspiring book.
* Going for a jog with a friend.
* Listening to beautiful music.
* A hug from someone I love.
* Giving myself positive input through motivational tapes.
* Chatting to my friends on the phone.

IF LIFE DEALS YOU LEMONS MAKE LEMONADE

The best antidote to depression is to laugh. Ask yourself, "Am I taking myself too seriously?" Keep yourself busy. Tidy cupboards, cook, garden, do errands for others. Make someone else happy. Try to see your problem in perspective. My greatest asset is the ability to laugh. When you laugh endorphins are released into your brain which give you a "natural high". Laughter relaxes you.

My favourite friends are the ones who make me laugh. I look for funny situations I can share. When I was jogging yesterday I saw the following bumper sticker: **If life deals you lemons make lemonade.**

HAVING A LOVE AFFAIR WITH LIFE

Life is a celebration. Are you holding a flickering match or letting off fireworks?

My life is always open to meet and accept new people, to become involved, to experience intensity and to share fun activities. I meet and befriend people anywhere, anytime. I think everybody has it in them to **be creative happy, successful and outgoing.** Selling releases many inhibitions and teaches you the skills of approaching strangers, being able to begin a conversation with a wide variety of people and enjoy the contact.

For me to get involved in a project or business, it has to make my heart beat faster, my adrenalin rise and leave me breathless **with passion and excitement**. I can't wait to wake in the morning so that I can continue to work on my project, when it's in my heart, head and blood, I know it's mine. I can give it all it takes to achieve success. This is how you have to feel about your business. The road to success has no room for doubts or anything less than total commitment.

The women achievers I talked to have those attitudes to their business: Love of people and zest for life.

Your new business in direct selling will **give you an exciting lifestyle**. You will have opportunities you never dreamed about.

Many companies have the possibility of **international sponsoring** and establishing a world-wide network. This option is limitless. It is exciting, stimulating and challenging. As we approach the 21st century we need to open our minds to a **global economy**. Boundaries and borders dissolve and international business becomes a reality for you and for me.

Helping others becomes a way of life for those active in this business. Technological advances enable us to sponsor people long distance. With facsimile machines, conference calls, mobile telephones, audio cassettes and videos, as well as the ease of travel, more and more leaders are able to reach further afield to expand their networks.

The best feedback an author can have is to be told something they have written has changed someone's life for the better.

In the few years since publishing my first book **There's a Lipstick in my Briefcase**, I have lectured extensively around Australia. I have returned many times to various cities. The most rewarding response from women has been the real change they have effected in their lives as a result of reading the book. **I hope this book will be a source of information, inspiration and encouragement as you develop your career in the direct selling industry.**

APPENDIX

GUIDE TO DIRECT SELLING COMPANIES

Aloette
Amway
Avon
Avroy Shlain
Beauty For All Seasons
Billicart
Elmon
Emma Page
Encyclopaedia Britannica
Fensmore
Forever Living
Herbalife
Jigsaw
Lady Remington
Learner's World
Le Reve
Mary Kay
Mini Minor
Nature's Sunshine
Neways
Nu Skin
Nutri-Metics
One Earth
Pola
Pro-Ma
Rawleigh
Reliv
Undercover Underwear
World Book

ALOETTE

Brian Pellerman
58 Cranbrook Road
ROSE BAY NSW 2029
Telephone: (02) 363 0626
Fax: (02) 326 2208

ALOETTE COSMETICS USA
345 Lancaster Avenue
MALVERN PA 19355 USA
Telephone: 215 644 8200
Fax: 215 644 5349

COMPANY HISTORY

Aloette was started in 1977 in Philadelphia by Tricia Defibaugh who developed a range of aloe-based cosmetics. It is now a public company earning more than $100 million in the US and $60 million in Canada each year. The company is a franchise organisation which makes it a little different in structure to other direct selling companies. Only women can be franchisees, however they can appoint managers of either sex.

PRODUCTS

Extensive range of aloe based skincare and makeup.

MARKETING PLAN

Sales of cosmetics are made through the party plan system. Aloette agents demonstrate the cosmetics and orders are placed directly with the franchisee who holds the stock.

AMWAY

AMWAY OF AUSTRALIA PTY LTD
Bruce Shankland
46 Carrington Road,
CASTLE HILL NSW 2154
Telephone: (02) 680 2222
Fax: (02) 680 2868

AMWAY CORPORATION USA
7575 Fulton Street
EAST ADA
MI 49355-0001 USA
Telephone: (616) 676 6000
Fax: (616) 676 6177

MISSION STATEMENT

"The Amway Corporation is dedicated to the spirit of free enterprise. The company seeks to forge lasting business relationships with forward thinking, ambitious and dedicated individuals who aspire to a better quality of life."

COMPANY HISTORY

The Amway Corporation was founded in 1959 by Jay Van Andel and Richard M Devos. Amway started by manufacturing a single household cleaner from a small building in Michigan (USA). The product Liquid Organic Cleaner (LOC) was so remarkable that the new company met with huge success and in a few years grew to become one of the world's great marketing stories.

Amway entered the Australian market in April 1971. It was the company's first venture outside North America. From humble beginnings in a small office, Amway of Australia now operates from impressive corporate headquarters in Castle Hill,

NSW. This combined office complex and full service regional distribution centre covers 13 acres and employs more than 350 peo ple whose primary role is to support Amway distributors and their business activities. The operational centre also offers customer advice, business development guidelines and training, sales marketing and product knowledge, legal and public relations support.

There are now more than 100,000 distributorships in Australia. Amway is unique in that over 95 per cent of the business builders are husband and wife teams.

Today Amway is one of Australia's top 500 companies with a retail turnover for 1991-1992 of $250 million. This represents an annual increase of 25 per cent.

This is a viable business opportunity with no need for capital or formal business qualifications. You can join for under $200 operate from your own home and enjoy the benefits of tax deductions through running your own business. Another attraction of the Amway business is that as its goodwill develops this asset can be sold or willed to someone else.

PRODUCTS

Amway products are renowned for their quality. The company's products outperform their competition and provide value for money. Amway endeavours to source or develop the best products in terms of performance and value for money in each product category.

Amway classics include liquid organic cleaner, S-A-8 laundry detergent Nutriway, personal care, cosmetics, jewellery, clothing, toys, housewares, plastic ware, microwave cookware, car and house security products and even food, juices and confectionery. The range grows weekly.

Amway are committed to giving a fair go to small business by supporting manufacturers of goods made and designed in Australia.

Amway has always taken a responsible role in relation to the environment, and makes a point of developing environmentally sensitive products and packaging.

PHILOSOPHY

Amway Corporation is a dynamic and growing international organisation dedicated to the "spirit of free enterprise". The company offers the potential of financial independence. It also offers the fulfilment gained from personal achievement and recognition from one's peers and business associates.

MARKETING PLAN

Amway is essentially a retail business. Both the business opportunity and the sales and marketing plan are both orientated towards retailing activities. Success is dependent on the development of a strong customer base. The company provides the products, the distributor builds and services the customers base. In essence it is the sale and use of products by customers and Amway distributors that generate income.

But Amway is not a traditional retailer and there is no conventional shop front. Amway has a unique personal in home service. This provides customers with a unique innovative and personalised way to shop without the hassles of traditional shopping such as parking, poor service or finding a babysitter for the children.

Amway distributors start by offering personalised service and exceptional products to friends, neighbours and regular acquaintances. However to develop a large business you need to establish more outlets for Amway products. This is done by sponsoring new distributors. You can build your business further by helping the people you sponsor to build their personal customer base and to recruit new distributors.

AVON

AVON PRODUCTS PTY LTD
Nigel Sinclair
120 Old Pittwater Road
BROOKVALE NSW 2100
Telephone: 938 8222
Fax: (02) 938 8310

AVON PRODUCTS INC.
Nine West S& Street
NEW YORK NY 10019 USA
Telephone: (212) 546 6015
Fax: (212) 546 6136

MISSION STATEMENT

"To re-establish Avon Australia as the leading information-driven beauty care and related products company in the direct channel, providing consumers with a wide range of excellent products in an environment and through a service which best suits their needs."

COMPANY HISTORY

Avon was started 105 years ago in the USA by David McConnell. The traditional Avon lady's catch cry, "Ding Dong Avon Calling" quickly became familiar to housewives throughout the world.

Avon has more than 30,000 consultants, almost all of whom are women selling products to other women. Avon ladies began door-to-door marketing in Australia in 1963. Avon Australia is currently turning over more than $114 rnillion.

Avon has the largest customer base of any direct se~ling company in Australia with sales representatives servicing 1.5 million customers. Of these 25 per cent of the sales are generated in offices and factories and the balance m the homes. Avon is now targeting the working woman.

PRODUCTS

Avon is undergoing dramatic changes. The company has just introduced new selling kits which include samples of many of Avon's cosmetics and a beauty computer that tells customers which colour cosmetics and skin care range they should use.

Avon's product range contains more than 1,000 items with cosmetics, toiletries and perfumes accounting for 65 per cent of the range. Toys, videos, clothing and fashion accessories account for the balance of the product. The Avon catalogue is the company's most powerful selling tool. Avon Australia issues 600,000, 80-100 page catalogues every three weeks.

PHILOSOPHY

The company believes in supporting women. Avon is committed to improving the quality of life for women and has many programs in place to recognise women's achievements.

MARKETING PLAN

Avon representatives rely on repeat sales for their business. Ideally in each three week cycle Avon representatives complete three tasks with each customer: They deliver goods ordered during the previous cycle, take orders for the present cycle and deliver brochures for the next cycle.

Avon has a $15 joining fee for new recruits and representatives are paid commissions on sales they generate. The highest commission is paid on cosmetics, toiletries and perfume. A lesser commission is paid on toys, apparel and videos. Avon does not have a multi-level remuneration scheme.

TRAINING

In Australia, Avon employs 110 district managers who are paid to sign new recruits, train and motivate new consultants and handle product orders and distribution.

A new beauty program gives half-day training in skin care and make up. A charge of $45 applies to these courses with the representative receiving a certificate and products at the end of the session.

AVROY SHLAIN

AVROY SHLAIN COSMETICS PTY LIMITED
PO Box 884
WENDYWOOD 2144, SOUTH AFRICA
Telephone: 011 444 2960
Fax: 444 1227, 444 3976

MISSION STATEMENT

To be conspicuously the best especially with regard to people and product. The company's overriding principle is that people are its key interest and major asset.

COMPANY HISTORY

Avroy Shlain was founded in South Africa in 1973 by Avroy and Beryl Shlain and now has 6000 consultants. The company plans to continue to expand in South Africa and throughout the world. It is already big in Israel and Zimbabwe and is growing in Switzerland, Belgium and Britain, and has a presence in Australia, Mauritius and Singapore.

PRODUCTS

A full range of cosmetic, skin care, fragrance and inner health products. All are of the highest international standards.

MARKETING PLAN

Beauty advisors report to group distributors who work in areas which are run by area distributors. They in turn report to their regional distributor who is in close contact with the corporate office.

TRAINING

Comprehensive quality training is given at every level of the organisation.

RECOGNITION, REWARDS, INCENTIVES

Avroy Shlain's sales force works for generous volume discounts on sales achieved. They also work for silver, gold and diamond awards and receive many other benefits including an overseas incentive trip.

BEAUTY FOR ALL SEASONS

BEAUTY FOR ALL SEASONS
Irene Wilson
Unit 30, 7 Salisbury Road
CASTLE HILL, NSW 2154
Telephone: (02) 899 2700
Fax: (02) 899 2307

BEAUTY FOR ALL SEASONS
Norma Virgin - CEO
360B St Idaho Falls
IDAHO 83405-1810 USA
Telephone: (208) 325 7880
Fax:(208) 325 7800

COMPANY HISTORY

In 1976, Norma Virgin started a small personal colour consulting business in Idaho Falls, Idaho. Today Beauty For All Seasons is an international leader in the science of personal image and personal colour analysis. The company has trained more than 18,000 consultants in the US and abroad. The Australian company was set up in 1984.

PRODUCTS

Beauty For All Seasons offers a full service beauty system which includes complete instruction on colours, skin care, make up and personal style. The company markets a complete line of seasonally co-ordinated make up and skin care products to complement and enhance the unique needs of each client.

MARKETING PLAN

Consultants start by receiving 40 per cent commission on the skin care and make up products, Signia and Imagio. A consultant can also practice as a trainer and can build an organisation.

TRAINING

Once a year consultants benefit from a three-day seminar conducted by one of Beauty for All Seasons' top international instructors.

RECOGNITION, REWARDS, INCENTIVES

Fabulous conferences at places such as Club Med. Consultants also receive numerous gifts and incentives for sponsoring recruits.

BILLICART

BILLICART CLOTHING PTY LTD
Denni Francisco, Niamh McCall
71 Hardiman Street
KENSINGTON VIC 3031
Telephone: (03) 372 2055
Fax: (03) 372 2026

MISSION STATEMENT

Billicart is an Australian company dedicated to global development through the strength of quality local partnerships that include staff, sales team, hosts, customers, suppliers, manufacturers and all those who help supply the company's unique service. The company's vision is fostered through a passionate commitment to the Billicart culture, recognition of achievement, respect for each individual and the reinforcement of family values.

COMPANY HISTORY

Billicart is a direct selling company that was started in 1989 by Denni Francisco and Niamh McCall. The company manufactures designer children's wear and offers a career alternative for women that gives them the flexibility to combine work with family life. The company comprises 50 people in the head office and a sales force of more than 600. Denni and Niamh started Billicart to provide a chance for women to work while still meeting family commitments. The company plans to expand overseas while continuing to build its strength in Australia.

PRODUCTS

Billicart has a range of fun clothing for children aged between three months and 14 years. The colours are strong and vibrant. Every garment complements all past and future Billicart designs so you can create a co-ordinated wardrobe for your children without breaking the family budget.

MARKETING PLAN

Sales are conducted in a party plan format. Every recruit starts as a sales executive. There is a structured career path that can lead them to become a branch manager and be eligible to earn a company car, overseas convention attendance, various sales incentives and monthly sales awards. Consultants are encouraged to recruit a team and earn an override commission.

Hostesses are invited to hold a range review. The hostess receives discounts and incentive gifts for sales made on the day. Your career begins when you buy a sample range which is offered at a 50 per cent discount on retail value. The kit becomes an investment which you sell at the end of the season before purchasing a new kit for the next season. Billicart can be a part time or full time commitment.

ELMON

ELMON

Theresa Spence
Suite 1, 16 Anella Avenue
CASTLE HILL, NSW 2154
Telephone: 02 680 1286
Fax: 02 894 6617

Box 40-185
Glenfield
AUCKLAND
Telephone: 9 443 6243
Fax: 9 443 6328

MISSION STATEMENT

To enhance people's living environment through the effective marketing of functionally designed quality products that are aesthetically pleasing and provide good value.

COMPANY HISTORY

Elmon is a privately owned and managed New Zealand registered company. The shareholders are Paul Reid, Irwin Stewart and Aaron Webber who are equal partners with specific line responsibilities.

Through clever niche marketing the company has developed an age-old concept by combining it with a modern marketing method to create an interest and demand previously unknown. In nine years, the company has grown from a small cottage industry to a market leader in its field of kitchen and dining decor with an annual turnover of more than $9 million. The company was set up in New Zealand and in 1987 expanded into Australia.

PRODUCT

Elmon prides itself in offering a unique product and service. The concept is one of service, quality, co-ordination and value for money. The company offers a wide variety of colour options and choices of colourful, co-ordinated kitchen, dining and laundry accessories. **The most attractive range of products consists of oven gloves, appliance covers, table cloths, serviettes and place mats.** There are more than 300 different product options with new colours, fabrics and designs introduced on a regular basis.

MARKETING PLAN

From 1984, Elmon made the decision to focus purely on **party plan sales**. The full scale party plan incorporates the following:

1. A commission sale force of more than 350 consultants
2. A field management organisation
3. Hostess rewards
4. Recruitment incentives
5. A comprehensive incentive program
6. Training systems and field support
7. Product innovation and development.

Elmon has a strong 'esprit de corps' among its people and is also highly regarded in the market place for its quality and commitment to service. The company is now poised with a success formula and plan that has universal application.

EMMA PAGE

EMMA PAGE PTY LTD
Raymond Vidor
30-32 Glenferrie Road
MALVERN VIC 3144
Telephone: 903) 576 0888
Fax: (03) 576 0556

MISSION STATEMENT

"It must be good and profitable for the other person before it can be good or profitable for me."

COMPANY HISTORY

Chairman Raymond Vidor founded Emma Page in Melbourne 23 years ago. The company now operates all states of Australia, New Zealand, Singapore and Malaysia and has offices in New York. All the jewellery is designed in New York. There is more than 1000 consultants promoting Emma Page. Its product is widely accepted, easy to sell and there is a high earning potential.

PRODUCTS

Emma Page manufactures more than 80 per cent of its products in New Zealand where the company has engaged the services of craftsmen formally trained in making jewellery. These fine tradesmen account for the superior quality of Emma Page's products. Emma Page designers travel the world several times a year to ensure an exclusive and dynamic range which is updated at least three times a year. Each item is covered by a written six month guarantee of free replacement.

MARKETING PLAN

Sales are based on the party plan concept and an average party of six guests would generate $350. Each hostess who achieves basic sales levels at any two party dates receives free, especially-designed reward pieces. Many hostesses become Emma Page consultants. Consultants earn commission on all retail sales plus bonuses for high performance. Consultants are able to buy Emma Page jewellery at a discount.

TRAINING

Free training is available on a weekly basis. Mangers are given special leadership training, rewards are by commission and management is earned by sales volume. Emma Page provides free professional training to help consultants start and develop their business. Training covers jewellery demonstrations, party bookings, sponsoring and basic business skills.

International conferences are organised annually at places such as Singapore, Bali, Hong Kong, Bangkok and Disneyland in California.

RECOGNITION, REWARDS AND INCENTIVES

The more time consultants devote to their business the more they earn. The aim in Emma Page is to gain the best financial rewards for time and efforts. When personal retail sales and team numbers grow to target levels, Emma Page offers a new car.

ENCYCLOPAEDIA BRITANNICA

ENCYCLOPAEDIA BRITTANICA AUST INC
Tom Gies
12 Annella Ave,
CASTLE HILL NSW 2154
Telephone:
Fax: (02) 899 3231

ENCYCLOPAEDIA BRITANNICA USA INC
Britannica Centre
310 South Michigan Avenue
CHICAGO Il 60604 USA
Telephone: (312) 347 7000
Fax: (312) 347 7399

COMPANY HISTORY

Encyclopaedia Britannica was first published in Edinburgh, Scotland in 1768 which was 20 years before Captain Cook came to Australia. It is the oldest continuously published encyclopaedia in the English language.

Britannica's offices and distributors are worldwide. For Australia and New Zealand, the company's head office is in Sydney with sales offices in every capital city and a number of regional centres. While the encyclopaedia remains the cornerstone of the company, Britannica is a leader in such diverse educational products as film, video tape, laser video discs and computer software as well as additional print publications including atlases and dictionaries.

PRODUCTS

For more than 200 years the name Britannica has been synonymous with education. The organisation is active in the publication of text books, dictionaries, elementary encyclopaedia and many other ventures. Britannica is a learning centre for the whole family. It is also the reference standard for the world.

MARKETING PLAN

Twenty-five per cent of the Encyclopaedia Britannica sales force is women. The company's aim is to increase that number. In Australia there are between 250 and 300 field sales agents who have a full time career within the company. To be successful you need to be self motivated. The big earners work hard and are rewarded for their efforts. Direct selling is not an easy fix. Encyclopaedia Britannica does not cold call. Each state sales office has a marketing manager reporting to the sales manager, to train agents in marketing techniques. Different methods are used to generate business such as untended display units that are set up with free draw entry cards to be filled out and returned to Britannica for the chance to win products and at the same time seek information.

RECOGNITION, REWARDS, INCENTIVES

To add incentive and encourage competition all Britannica agents enter regular company contests that include rewards such as overseas travel. They also co-operate with special promotions. Britannica promotes from within. You can move through the ranks from field manager to area, district and division manager.

FENSMORE

FENSMORE PTY LTD
Steve McNamee
18 Roseberry Road
KELLYVILLE, NSW
Telephone: (02) 629 2311
Fax: 629 2122

MISSION STATEMENT

To continue to ensure Fensmore remains the premier **plant party company** in the country by retaining a high standard of both product and service and through the introduction of new appropriate products in the future.

COMPANY HISTORY

Fensmore was established in 1975 and began selling hydroculture plants in 1979. There are 600 sales consultants throughout Australia.

PRODUCTS

Indoor hydroculture plant kits for growing indoor plants and living plants growing in hydroculture kits. There is also a range of accessories that includes nutrient, fungicide, insecticide, wall clips, hangers and garden lights.

MARKETING PLAN

Fensmore works on a multilevel marketing and networking plan and has a complete party plan incentive program for hosts. **The special thing about this opportunity is that it offers the benefits of both multilevel marketing and party plan.**

TRAINING

Full training is given free to active consultants. Training is based on a 150 page manual, weekly, fortnightly and monthly meetings and on the job training at presentations.

FOREVER LIVING

FOREVER LIVING PRODUCTS AUSTRALIA PTY LIMITED
Vince Rimmer
PO Box 480
BAULKHAM HILLS, NSW 2153
Telephone: (02) 624 5599
Fax: (02) 624 6782

MISSION STATEMENT

Healthy lifestyle and financial freedom.

COMPANY HISTORY

Forever Living was formed in the US 15 years ago and is privately owned by Rex Maughan. In 1991 the company generated sales exceeding $500 million which was a 90 per cent growth over 1990. In 1992 the company generated sales of more than $600 million based on retail. Forever Living is now in 25 countries and is the **world's largest grower, producer and distributor of aloe vera.** The company recently bought Southfork Ranch of Dallas TV fame which will be the site of the 1993 convention.

The company has been established for ten years in Australia and has offices in every state. There are 2000 active distributors.

PRODUCTS

Skin care and health products made from aloevera.

MARKETING PLAN

No joining fee. Bonuses are paid on a figure greater than wholesale. There is a 30 per cent mark up at all levels. Bonuses of five per cent to 18 per cent on personal sales with overrides ranging from two per cent to nine per cent. There are overseas trips and cash incentives.

TRAINING

Weekly training meetings on product and business building.

HERBALIFE

HERBALIFE AUSTRALASIA PTY LTD
Bob Holdsworth
64 George Street
Thebarton SA 5031
Telephone: (08) 301 6066
Fax: (08) 352 6564

HERBALIFE INTERNATIONAL
Mark Hughes
9800 Le Cienega Blvd
PO Box 80210
LOS ANGELES LA 90009 USA
Telephone: (213) 410 9600
Fax: (213) 216 7454

MISSION STATEMENT

To provide better nutrition and health to the world.

COMPANY HISTORY

Herbalife was established in 1980 by the company's president Mark Hughes. Mark was at the time in his early 20s. He is a man of vision and determination. His dream was to bring better nutrition to as many people as quickly as possible throughout the world.

The company's headquarters is in Los Angeles, but Herbalife operates in 16 countries with annual sales of more than US$500 million. Herbalife's products were developed by a biochemist and a team of four doctors.

In Australia where the company has been operating since 1983, there are over 15,000 distributors. Annual sales in Australia are around $20 million.

PRODUCTS

The product range contains nutritional products as well as skin and hair care. The Diet Disc formula is nutritious way to lose weight in conjunction with a calorie-controlled diet. The diet program includes fibre supplements, vitamins and minerals. The herbal skin care, herbal aloe vera gel, herbal shampoo and tanning lotion are in the skin care range.

MARKETING PLAN

Herbalife has a five-step marketing plan. When you join the company you start as a distributor. Through sponsoring and expanding your team and retail sales, you become a supervisor. You then become part of the tabulator team which has three levels, national expansion team, millionaire team and president's team.

PHIILOSOPHY

The company aims to help customers obtain their desired goal weight and better health and well being on a continuing basis and not just a short term basis.

TRAINING

The company provides training through weekly meetings, conference calls, work manuals and leadership weekends. Training is mostly free and world class trainers are brought in to teach and inspire business builders.

RECOGNITION, REWARDS, INCENTIVES

A special technique used by Herbalife is to build your own story bank by getting as many customers on the product as you can. You are encouraged to follow up, get repeat orders and gain referrals.

Plan for success:
- Use the products seriously every day. This is critical in the first 90-days because your belief in the product will hold you to the company while you are building your business.
- Lose weight and feel healthier. Get others to lose weight.
- Wear the company button. Sincerity sells.
- Make a list of everyone you know.
- Sponsor wide and deep.
- Qualify for supervisor as fast as possible.

JIGSAW TOY FACTORY

JIGSAW TOY FACTORY
Jeanie McKendrick
14 Palmer Court
MT WAVERLEY VIC 3149
Telephone: (03) 544 4344
Fax: (03) 543 7320

MISSION STATEMENT

"This business is dedicated to the ultimate benefit of children everywhere." Jigsaw believes children learn through play and that toys are vital tools in their growth and development.

COMPANY HISTORY

Jigsaw is entirely Australian owned and operated. The company was started in the early 1970s by a group of creative people headed by two top graphic designers. In 1974, Jeanie McKendrick took over the company and direct selling was chosen as the best method of marketing. "The Toy Shop With A Difference, The Toy Shop That Comes To You" was born.

PRODUCTS

Jigsaw is a recognised leader in the specialised field of **educational games and toys.** The greatest percentage of the company's products are manufactured in Australia to original designs.

MARKETING PLAN

The only way to see the exclusive range of educational games and toys is at a **Talkabout.** Talkabouts are held in schools, kindergartens, playgroups and the home. The Jigsaw sales person is known as a product adviser. The party plan concept is used for the Talkabout.

The Jigsaw business opportunity allows an adviser to create a career that is fun, exciting and financially rewarding. Jigsaw can be a part time career or a full time business. Product advisers progress through levels of management to executive manager.

TRAINING

Jigsaw's aim has always been to match its outstanding products with outstanding people and to this end great emphasis is placed on training. Regular seminars and workshops throughout Australia cover product knowledge, child development and sales techniques.

LADY REMINGTON

Elizabeth and Gary Miller
14 Main Street
OSBORNE PARK WA
Telephone: (09) 444 4936
Fax: (09) 444 4092

John Kiple - CEO
818 Thorndale Avenue
Bensenville ILLINOIS 60106 USA
Telephone: 708 860 3323
Fax: 708 860 5634

MISSION STATEMENT

To create service, quality and opportunities that build people.

COMPANY HISTORY

This company was founded in 1971. In 1986 the company was bought by Victor Kiam. Lady Remington is an aggressive, stable, well-financed company with extensive plans for growth both in Australia and overseas. Currently the company operates in the US, Australia, New Zealand, Singapore, Greece and it will soon be in Mexico and Canada.

John Kiple has been president since 1977. In 1988 Elizabeth and Gary Miller were appointed directors of Lady Remington Australia with the responsibility for importing, marketing and developing the product and service throughout the country. In the past five years, Lady Remington has seen enormous growth.

PRODUCTS

High quality, exciting fashion jewellery. There are 150 consultants active in Australia and more than 2000 in the US, Singapore and New Zealand.

MARKETING PLAN

Products are sold by party plan. Consultants get 25 per cent commission on retail sales. The company pays hostesses with a generous gift program. Managers can earn override commissions on their team as well as bonuses. There are incentive gifts, trips and generous reward systems in place. Lady Remington is a special company where managers are financially rewarded for developing managers for their group.

TRAINING

Comprehensive field training, manuals, videos and regular meetings. Consultants are encouraged to sponsor with both financial rewards as well as free jewellery as prizes. An opportunity exists for promotion based on performance.

LEARNER'S WORLD

LEARNER'S WORLD
David Brownlow
235 Bay Road
CHELTENHAM, VIC 3192
Telephone: (03) 553 4538
Fax: (03) 555 1344

MISSION STATEMENT

Bringing out the best.

COMPANY HISTORY

While he was teaching in Tasmania in the '70s many of David Brownlow's friends would seek his advice on which were the best educational toys to buy their children.

That's where the idea for Learner's World was first developed and the company started operating in Tasmania and Victoria in 1979.

The dream was to provide parents with the **best educational toys, games and books** so their children's lives could be enriched and their educational experiences broadened. Initially Learner's World created and manufactured many of its games and toys, some of which are still sold. In searching for the best toys available the company began looking overseas. Today the range includes Australian-designed and manufactured products and some of the best toys from the US, Europe, Asia and New Zealand.

PRODUCTS

The Learner's World product range is made up of more than 170 individual items. There are educational books, games or toys for babies, toddlers, preschoolers and children in the primary and early secondary years. All products are exclusive to Learner's World and are made to the highest possible quality. They are all guaranteed.

MARKETING PLAN

Through recruiting and sales, demonstrators are able to increase their personal sales commission within a short time of joining the company. Promotion is available to all demonstrators once they have achieved excellent personal sales, are able to recruit and have leadership skills. The Learner's World career plan offers all demonstrators a five-tiered system from manager leading up to sales directors. Sales are made at party demonstrations.

TRAINING

From the moment every new demonstrator joins the company the management team makes available training opportunities.

RECOGNITION, REWARDS, INCENTIVES

The company provides a number of incentive programs. Attractive prizes include personal items, household, company stationery, samples of news products and overseas travel.

LE REVE

LE REVE COSMETICS PTY LTD
PO Box 2697
NORTH PARRAMATTA
NSW 2151 Australia
Telephone: (61 2) 683 2277
Fax:(61 2) 689 4473

MISSION STATEMENT

The good things are even better with Le Reve. Every once in a while all the right ingredients come together to produce success: The right people, the right idea and the right timing. Le Reve believes if you look good you'll feel good.

COMPANY HISTORY

Le Reve is a fully Australian-owned company that started in 1988. In less than five years of operation projected turnover is more than $5 million in sales. There are more than 2000 sales consultants.

The company is owned equally by Phillip Hobby and Richard Morse who have had many years experience in the direct selling business and are regularly both out in the field training directors and consultants. The company philosophy centres on leadership and a win-win attitude. The driving force is not dollars, but people's development.

PRODUCTS

Le Reve have a range of Collection Classique perfumes, bodysilks and fragrant dusting powder. The concept of layering encourages customers to buy their favourite fragrance in all three forms.

Le Reve also have a new skin care range called Collection Botanique. This range has been formulated by the president of the Australian Society of Cosmetic Chemists, Ray Townsend; one of Australia's best known medical herbalists, Penelope Sach; and a foremost beauty therapist and owner of a leading beauty therapy academy, Shirley Strickland. It is a safe, gentle skin care range that is 100 per cent fragrance free, not tested on animals, free of alcohol and artificial colours and free of animal ingredients and by-products. All products are beautifully packaged and presented.

MARKETING PLAN

Le Reve has combined the strengths of a party plan method of selling and multi-level remuneration. Royalties continue indefinitely. There are powerful incentives that include cars, overseas travel, conferences and retirement options. The business you build up can be sold or willed.

MARY KAY COSMETICS

MARY KAY COSMETICS PTY LTD
Brad Wright
551 Burwood Highway,
KNOXFIELD VIC 3180
Telephone: (03) 8016244
Fax: (03) 8013092

MARY KAY COSMETICS
Richard Bartlett
8787 Stemmond Fwy
DALLAS TX 75247 USA
Telephone: (214) 630 8787
Fax: (214) 638 4755

MISSION STATEMENT

"Praise people to success", is the doctrine of Mary Kay. "Make me feel important" is the cornerstone of the company's philosophy.

COMPANY HISTORY

There are 5,000 Mary Kay beauty consultants in Australia the company is doing annual sales in excess of $23 million in Australia and New Zealand.

Mary Kay is an enormously successful company in the USA where it began in 1963. **It provides an opportunity for more than 400,000 women and achieves yearly sales of over US$1 billion.**

There are 120 sales directors in Mary Kay Australia, and three national directors. Many consultant's are former professionals from careers in nursing and teaching and as secretaries.

PRODUCTS

Mary Kay has a very loyal customer base. The products have an excellent reputation for quality and effectiveness and are fully guaranteed. The product is delivered directly to the consultant within 24 hours from the receipt of an order.

PHILOSOPHY

The company was created so any woman could become successful. **Any woman could compete against her own best effort**. Each woman could become as successful as she wanted.

The company's objective is to give women the opportunity to do anything they were smart enough to do. In this company P and L mean more than **profit and loss, it means people and love**. In 1963 Mary Kay offered women opportunities that didn't exist anywhere else. Even today the vast majority of companies do not make room for women. Countless, capable individuals are held back only because they are female.

In Ma v Kav there are no territones he company focuses on "giving" not just "getting". It uses this philosophy in every aspect of the company. It is particularly true of customer relations. Consultants ask themselves what they can do for their customers that will make them feel better about themselves.

The philosophy of Golden Rule, "do unto others as we would have others do unto us" is the foundation of Mary Kay's business.

MARKETING PLAN

The beauty showcase start up kit costs $175 and contains $400 worth of cosmetics, literature and a full starter kit. Products are sold by consultants at **skin care classes** not parties or shows. With your first order Mary Kay sends you a free fast start product bonus to the value your showcase.

The company maintains a professional image and the **consultant becomes a skin care teacher**. Consultants earn according to the amount of time they invest. They have no quota, no areas or territories. They operate according to the "go-give" spirit. This means each director will take care of the beauty consultants in her area regardless of whether or not she is receiving direct commission from her sales. A consultant can sell anywhere in Australia and can attend training meetings conducted by any director throughout the country.

RECOGNITION, REWARDS, INCENTIVES

Consultants are encouraged to share the opportunity and are rewarded on new consultant sales with commissions and prizes such as pink cars, diamond jewellery and overseas trips.

The company's generous commission structure is in line with Mary Kay's belief that women should be highly rewarded for effort. Every May Kay consultant is an independent business person.

MINI MINORS

MINI MINOR PTY LTD
Sally Berkeley
Unit 149/313 Harris Street
ULTIMO NSW 2007
Telephone: (02) 552 3055
Fax: (02) 692 9782

MISSION STATEMENT

To provide a unique collection of children's wear each season while maintaining the highest possible standard of quality, design and service at an affordable price. A minimum of 85 per cent of the Mini Minors' range is under $40. Mini Minors aims to be the best in its business.

COMPANY HISTORY

Mini Minors was started in October 1990 by designer and entrepreneur Sally Berkeley. Sally is a young mother and a very creative, talented and dynamic businesswoman. Mini Minors have a customer base of more than 12,000 clients and 70 sales consultants. It is a new company that provides and exciting opportunity with an exclusive range of children's clothing.

PRODUCTS

Designer babies, children's wear, clothing and accessories for three months to eight years. Three new collections are released each year.

MARKETING PLAN

Clothes are sold in a **party plan** program. Unlike most direct selling organisations, Mini Minors offers area exclusivity. Mini Minors provides advertising and promotion assistance to all sales executives. There is a multi-level system of remuneration. Building of a network team is the path to financial success in this business. There are two levels sales executives: An individual concentrates on personal sales or sales manager who establishes an area and goes on to sponsor other sales representatives.

TRAINING

Product launches and demonstrations seminars are held three times a year. A step by step presentation video is available. Individual training, guidance and counselling are provided.

NATURE'S SUNSHINE

NATURE'S SUNSHINE
Stephen Webster
Unit 2, 360 Vardy's Road
MARAYONG, NSW 2148
Telephone: (02) 231 3233
Fax: (02) 231 2524

NATURE'S SUNSHINE PRODUCTS
Alan Kennedy
1655 North Main
P.O. Box 1000 Spanish Fork
UT 84660 USA
Telephone: 801 798 9861
Fax: 801 798 2730

MISSION STATEMENT

The company's philosophy is based on strong principles of commitment and a natural, commonsense approach to good health.

COMPANY HISTORY

Nature's Sunshine is a US-based company that manufactures a variety of nutritional and personal care products. The company was founded in 1972 by Kristine and Eugene Hughes who were seeking to feel better through improved nutrition.

PRODUCTS

Nutritional and personal care products including encapsulated herbs, vitamins, food **supplements**, Moritz skin care and colour products and Nature's spring water treatment systems.

MARKETING PLAN

Products are sold directly to consumers by means of an independent sales force throughout the US, Canada, New Zealand, the UK, Mexico, Colombia and Australia. It is a network marketing program in which distributors can earn money by selling products themselves and by inviting others to participate in the business. Nature's Sunshine is a recognised leader in the nutrition and natural health care industry. Today there are more than 130 single and combination herbal products available in the range. There are more than 2,600 distributors in Australia, of whom 165 are managers. The products are also sold by naturopaths and in health food stores. Sales in Australia exceed $3 million a year. In the US sales are more than $100 million a year with extensive growth in Hispanic countries. A starter kit costs $50 which includes audio cassette tapes, business material, brochures and access to product training.

Income is earned in three ways:
1. **Retail sales.** All distributors are entitled to buy at wholesale from the company and resell at retail.
2. Distributors earn **bonuses** on personal sales.
3. As you climb the levels of personal achievement, you begin to earn manager **override commissions** up to four levels.

RECOGNITION, REWARDS, INCENTIVES

Nature's Sunshine provides exciting, comprehensive benefits and incentive programs.

NEWAYS

NEWAYS INTERNATIONAL
Michael Cunningham
162 Fullerton Road
ROSEPARK, SA 5067
Telephone: (08) 364
Fax: (08) 364

NEWAYS INC
Tom and Dee Mower
150 East 400 North
SALEM Utah, 84653, USA
Telephone: (801) 423 2800
Fax: (801) 423 2350

MISSION STATEMENT

"To pursue our best in all facets of life and to help others do the same."

HISTORY OF COMPANY

Neways was started in March 1987 in Utah by Thomas Mower who was a research chemist. Neways began in Australia in 1989. The head office is in Adelaide. Currently there are 10,000 sales consultants in the company with an increase of about 130 per month. Sales for the 1993 calendar are anticipated to reach $40 million. Neways formulates, manufactures, packages and distributes its own products. Neways is debt free and soundly managed. The company prides itself on a high degree of corporate integrity and is vitally concerned with the environment.

The company plans to expand into south-east Asia and Europe. Neways are continually developing products that are safe and effective.

PRODUCTS

The exclusive product line is based upon the extensive research of Thomas Mower. The products are continually refined and improved to bridge the gap between science and human needs. The products cover six major groups: **skin, hair and nail care, body contouring, personal care, health and nutrition.**

All Neways products are unique, consumable, competitively priced, biodegradable and packaged in recyclable containers. Neways has won an award for not using animal testing. The company has a philosophy of product integrity which means no mineral oil, no collagen, no glycerin, no human placental extracts, no propylene glycol and no sodium lauryl sulphate are used. All products are highly consumable and provide the largest market as they **target the baby boomers** (ie those born between 1946 and 1964).

MARKETING PLAN

Neways is an MLM company whereby you are in business for yourself but not by yourself. Neways has an extremely generous marketing plan. Benefits include a direct ordering system from the company, 48-hour delivery turnaround, no bookwork, international sponsoring, retirement programs, you cannot be passed, your bonus cheque is all yours and once and rank is achieved, you never drop back.

TRAINING

- Free regular national business opportunity meetings
- Distributor advisory board
- Free product training
- Free business training

- Audio and video tapes
- Sales aids

RECOGNITION, REWARDS, INCENTIVES

- Car of your dreams
- Group volume bonuses
- International conventions
- Tax benefits
- Leadership bonuses are paid eight levels down.

Timing is to network marketing what location is to real estate. Time is everything. Neways Australia is about to enter an exciting growth phase.

NU SKIN

NU SKIN
Ron Innis
Unit 1, 14 Anella Avenue
CASTLE HILL NSW 2154
Telephone: (02) 899 9100
Fax: (02) 894 5244

NU SKIN
Blake M. Roney (President and CEO)
75 West Center Street
PROVO UTAH 848601 U.S.A.
Telephone: (801) 345 1000
Fax: (801) 345 3999

MISSION STATEMENT

All of the good, none of the bad. Nu Skin is a dynamic, rapidly growing company in the personal care industry. Nu Skin continues to improve the quality of people's lives with the highest quality products and unparalleled financial opportunity.

COMPANY HISTORY

The success of Nu Skin International Inc is a story of innovation, commitment to excellence, quality products and dedicated personal service. The Nu Skin vision of high quality personal care products without harmful fillers, was first conceived at a kitchen table by Nu Skin president Blake Roney and his sister. They decided to create a line of skin care products that contained only ingredients known to be beneficial.

The first shipment arrived in 1984. Nu Skin was in business. Having begun with less than $5000 start up capital, Nu Skin remains debt free. **Nu Skin is now a multi-million dollar company with world wide sales tipped to exceed $1 billion in 1993.**

Roney chose a network marketing and distribution system to market his products. As Nu Skin's sales grew, so did its product line.

Nu Skin began international operations in Canada in 1990 and has since moved into Hong Kong, Taiwan, Australia and New Zealand with plans to enter other Pacific rim countries, Europe, Mexico and Japan during the next few years.

In October 1992 Nu Skin launched a new division, **Interior Design Nutritionals** (IDN). Sales of nutritionals in the US are currently 40 per cent of the total sales. Plans are in hand to launch IDN in Australia later in 1993.

PRODUCTS

Nu Skin offers more than 60 products and the search for excellence has not ended. A multi-million dollar state-of-the-art laboratory was built during the first part of 1992 in Provo, Utah which is also home to the company's headquarters. **Nu Skin provides high quality products to the most important consumer segment today, the baby boomers.**

Blake Roney determined Nu Skin products would evolve as new and improved ingredients were discovered. Already many new technologies have been incorporated. Besides being scientifically innovative, Nu Skin contains many natural products such as Aloevera, vitamins A, B, C and E, royal jelly, jojoba and many herbs. Nu Skin products are allergy dermatologist tested and employ no harmful colouring agents, fragrances, alcohol or lanolin derivatives. **The range contains skin care, hair care, cleansers, conditioners, and sun protectors.**

MARKETING PLAN

Nu Skin has developed the most generous marketing system available. Network marketing is the only promotional and distribution channel utilised. **It combines excellent product with a superb sales compensation plan for a win win formula.** It allows you to be your own boss, work your own hours and determine you own destiny. The sales compensation plan provides distributors with a remarkable opportunity to earn money by retailing exceptional products. **Nu Skin bases its business on three principles: commitment, integrity and training others to do the same.** You receive a profit on retail sales plus bonuses from the sales of those you train to retail and recruit. Nu skin offers an opportunity to build an international network on a continuous, seamless basis.

TRAINING AND SUPPORT

- Corporate seminars (6 per year)
- Comprehensive product training manuals
- Regular distributor meetings
- Newsletters
- Corporate quarterly magazine

NUTRI-METICS

NUTRI-METICS INTERNATIONAL
(AUSTRALIA) PTY LTD
William Roche, Imelda Roche
102 Elliot Street,
BALMAIN NSW 2041
Telephone: (02) 818 9011
Fax: (02) 810 2838

NUTRI-METICS INC.
Mulford J. Nobbs
19501 East Walnut Drive
City of Industry
CALIFORNIA CA 91749 USA
Telephone: (714) 598 1831
Fax: (714) 595 3219

COMPANY HISTORY

Imelda Roche and her husband Bill started the Australian subsidiary of the then US-based Nutri-Metics International in 1968.

In 1991 the Roches took over the company world-wide. Today Nutri-Metics International which has branches in 15 countries, is run from the Roche's corporate head office in Balmain, Sydney.

In Australia, Nutri-Metics has an annual turn over of more than $150 million and an average annual growth of more than 20 per cent.

PHILOSOPHY

When she started the company, it was Imelda's goal to be the leading skin care company in Australia. She has achieved her goal and much more. The opportunities now offered to Nutri-Metics consultants around the world opens a whole new dimension to their businesses, consultants being able to expand into almost any of the 15 countries where Nutri-Metics is established. They have the opportunity to build global enterprises.

PRODUCTS

High in the Hunza Valley of the Himalayan mountains, the inhabitants use apricot kernel oil to protect their face, throat and hands from the elements. These people have complexions the envy of people half their age. The health and beauty properties of the remarkable apricot are nature's inspiration for Nutri-Metics. Nutri-Metics manufactures a range of naturally-enriched, hypo-allergenic skin care and beauty products. **All products are made with pure, safe, natural ingredients**. Two ranges make up a full skin care program. There is also a hair care range, fragrance, men's toiletries, sun care, a range of vitamins, minerals and food supplements, a wide variety of colour cosmetics and personal care items as well as a new range of health products.

All products are attractively packaged in pastel apricot tones. They are created without the use of animal testing and are safe, gentle and kind to sensitive skins.

MARKETING PLAN

The company is structured along classic direct selling lines. Consultants network among friends and relatives and sell the Nutri-Metics range in relaxed show plan setting. Each Nutri-Metics consultant is encouraged to focus on retail sales but the real rewards go to those who expand the sales force and earn commission on those they sponsor.

Only about ten per cent of the 100,000 or more consultants in Australia earn their living from Nutri-Metics. Most either use the products or earn part time money to supplement their existing incomes.

As consultants sign up more recruits they build a team and start to climb the rungs of management. The first level is director of which there are about 800. From there they move to district director, then regional director and finally to senior regional director of which there are 40 in Australia. **The senior regionals are a group of very successful women. They are leaders, achievers and role models for the 100,000 consultants in the field.**

RECOGNITION, REWARDS, INCENTIVES

The Nutri-Metics profit recognition plan provides exciting incentives and awards for achievers at all levels. It also **affords ordinary people the chance to lead extraordinary lives through unlimited potential income, international travel and luxury cars.**

"Nutri-Metics is more than just a skin care company," says Imelda Roche. "It's a lifestyle. It's a company that emphasises people by offering unparalleled opportunities for success, financial freedom, security and personal growth."

ONE EARTH (FORMERLY L'AROME)

ONE EARTH AUSTRALIA
John Lash
79a Egerston Road
SILVERWATER, NSW 2141
Telephone: (02) 748 3280
Fax: (02) 748 4282

ONE EARTH NEW ZEALAND
Mr H K Kok
77 Grafton Road
Parnell, AUCKLAND
Telephone: (09) 358 3888
Fax: (09) 302 2739

COMPANY HISTORY

One Earth (formerly (L'Arome) was founded in England in 1987 by four entrepreneurs who in a very short time reached sales of $40 million. The company set up in New Zealand in 1988 and in Australia in 1989. In Australia, there are more than 3,000 active consultants reaching annual sales of $7.8 million.

PRODUCTS

One Earth products comprise a line of fine fragrances and toiletries for women and men. The fragrances are available in various forms so you can enjoy using the layering effect of using more than one product. One Earth has also introduced a weight control system designed to control weight and maintain health. The formula comes in two superb-tasting flavours, chocolate and vanilla. The company also sells Royal Jelly. This has been used by many cultures through the ages and is attributed with increasing mental alertness, concentration and energy, and with reducing stress and tension. One Earth has introduced an Ecopure water filtration system and is developing a skin care line.

MARKETING PLAN

The One Earth system begins with consultant, then field manager, team manager, marketing director, regional marketing director up to executive director. The company has a highly profitable commission system that is a combination of wholesale commission and director commissions six levels deep. Executive directors receive bonuses.

POLA

POLA COSMETICS (AUSTRALIA) PTY LTD
Marcia Griffin
31 Wellington Street
WINDSOR VIC 3181
Telephone: (03) 529 5433
Fax: (03) 529 5989

POLA USA
251 East Victoria Avenue
CARSEN CA 90146
Telephone: (213) 770 6000
Fax: (213) 515 1195

MISSION STATEMENT

'To be **in business for yourself, not by yourself.'** Pola is committed to the ideal of beauty, customer satisfaction and service.

COMPANY HISTORY

Pola Cosmetics is one of the **world's largest cosmetics companies** with a turnover of around $2 billion. Pola was established in 1929. It is based in Tokyo,

Japan and is acclaimed as a leader in scientific research and quality control. The first ten years of Pola Australia have been dedicated to establishing a solid viable base. The next ten years will see accelerated growth. The company offers rapid promotion for those with a commitment to success.

Through the development of the most advanced products available, Pola has determined that direct marketing is the most effective way to ensure personal attention and service from it network of trained consultants. Marcia Griffin who is general manager of Pola Australia says Pola is the number one direct selling cosmetic company in Japan and number two in the world. Pola has more than 200,000 consultants world wide with more than six million customers.

PRODUCTS

Pola has 300 researchers and spends $100 million each year on research to bring you a range of **quality skin care products and cosmetics.** Pola provides a total guarantee with each product. Products are designed to last a long time. They represent value and the range is continually upgraded.

MARKETING PLAN

Pola consultants come from all walks of life, some are teachers, lawyers, housewives, nurses, secretaries, make up artists, beauty therapists and hairdressers. **Products are sold either one on one with the customer or at product demonstrations.** The opportunity to be promoted from a consultant to manager is open to all. Success and effort are well rewarded. Customers are provided with samples and free facials. At each group presentation the hostess receives a free facial, ten per cent commission and other benefits (at least $100 and free product of choice).

Consultants receive excellent bonuses on sales of their recruits and successes in team building and leveraging time by teaching others to develop their businesses.

TRAINING

All Pola consultants have the chance of comprehensive company training. This introduces the consultant to a proven method of establishing client business as well as a full program of skin care and product knowledge. Consultants are also given regular ongoing management training with the company. **Incentives include exciting international travel to fabulous destinations.**

PRO-MA

PRO-MA SYSTEMS
(AUST) PTY LTD
Val P. Fittler
151 Currumburra Road,
ASHMORE QLD 4214
Telephone: (075) 396 366
Fax: (075) 395 965

PRO-MA SYSTEMS (USA) INC.
Gene Rumley
477 Commerce Way
Suite 1113LONGWOOD
FL 32752-2109 USA
Telephone: (407) 331 1133
Fax: (407) 331 1125

MISSION STATEMENT

"We believe in people and their dreams and their unlimited potential to achieve them."

COMPANY HISTORY

The managing director of Pro-Ma Systems, Val Fittler is an inspiring man. He started the company in 1983 with Pro-Ma Performance Products, a range of car care products and a year later introduced Grace Cosmetics.

Val Fittler's vision is to offer a quality range of products, an effective marketing plan and he places great importance on training. Val has been a student of personal development for 22 years. He is a field-oriented leader.

The whole Fittler family is involved in the business. Val's wife Sandra handles staff, product development and promotions, his daughter Julie is international sales director and Julie's husband is in advertising and promo tion. Val's youngest daughter works the company's public relations. Through their activities the family knows almost all of the many thousands of active dis tributors by name.

PRODUCTS

Pro-Ma System's products are divided into three divisions, **Pro-Ma Systems car care and car performance products, Grace Cosmetics** and a new division of nutritional products, **Pro-Ma Nutrition.**

Val Fittler has spent many years researching health and fitness products. He now has a formula which caters for the specific needs of men and women and which includes a weight management program of made up of a fibre product to reduce the appetite, a spray of natural herbs that restores the balance of the blood sugar level and a formula of vitamins and minerals.

Grace Cosmetics are based on aloe and all essential vitamins and are water soluble. The skin care range has built in sun protection. The philosophy behind the cosmetics is to make women feel better about themselves and to create inner and outer beauty.

PHILOSOPHY

"Our dreams can come true if we have the courage to pursue them."

Pro-Ma encourages consultants to stretch themselves to give more, to do more and to reach out to others. The company believes money is only a tool and is neither good or evil in itself, but if managed well money can bring enjoyment of some of the finer things in life. Pro-Ma also encourages consultants to free themselves from debt.

MARKETING PLAN

Consultants are encouraged to build a team through networking as well as to continue to retail the products through servicing their customers.

There is a large number of directors in the company. From the level of director they can moved into the level of senior director, Gold Senior and executive director. There are more than 20 executive directors in Australia.

Over and above building a network, there is a chance to participate in field management. There are national and regional managers in each country of operation. Directors can attain these positions after they have built a network. Field managers support directors and consultants in developing their businesses.

TRAINING

The Fittler family works closely in the field with its consultants to give personal development and management skills, leadership strategies, selling skills and after sales service for customers. They do not charge the consultants for training. They also give consultants a training manual, audio and video material.

Pro-Ma focuses on the individual, to build a better person. Workshops are provided on skin care, colour imaging and intensive workshops for women on self-esteem and personal growth.

RECOGNITION, REWARDS, INCENTIVES

At both state and national levels the creative awards are designed for consultants to display their skill, creativity, flair and individuality. Finalists receive travel prizes and a chance to explore new dimensions of confidence, personal growth and initiative.

Pro-Ma has launched a new recognition program, the Rewards Club which will recognise and reward the performance of its distributors with quality merchandise, overseas travel, computers or a new car.

I had the privilege to be a guest at the Pro Ma 1992 international conven tion on the Gold Coast. The theme was "Nothing Is Impossible". With the excitement, enthusiasm and energy at Pro-Ma, I got the feeling that nothing was impossible!

RAWLEIGH

RAWLEIGH PTY LTD	W.T. RAWLEIGH
Beau Moller	P.O. Box 38009
Unit 4, 29 Victoria Avenue	PETONE
CASTLE HILL NSW 2154	Wellington
Telephone: (02) 634 7600	Telephone (4) 69 1116
Fax: (02) 899 1865	Fax: (4) 69 6532

MISSION STATEMENT

'A friend of the family since 1889'. Since the late 1880s, Rawleigh have promoted the following principles:

1. Sell quality products direct to consumers in their homes.

2. Provide people with an opportunity to own a profitable, independent retailing business.

COMPANY HISTORY

WT Rawleigh Company was started in the US by William Thomas Rawleigh when he was 18. This farmer's son from Wisconsin was fired with the ambition to get into medicine. He started with a borrowed horse, a mortgaged buggy and a line of liniment, condition powders, stick salve, pills, and lemon and vanilla extracts. The company had to be sold after Rawleigh's death in 1951. In 1992, Terry Rawleigh, WT's great grandson bought the company and rejuvenated the marketing plan by adopting multi-level marketing techniques. There are 4020 distributors in Australia and a turnover of $8million.

PRODUCTS

The current Rawleigh range of more than 170 items includes **personal care products, medicinal, household and gourmet food products, spices, essences, vitamins, cosmetics and perfumes, desserts, skin care, low calorie juices, helath bread and milk.** The packaging is reminiscent of times past with very fashionable, traditional labelling. About half of the products are made in Australia and half in New Zealand. There is an unconditional guarantee on all products.

MARKETING PLAN

Research has shown a greater proportion of the community would **rather shop at home.** There is therefore a very real opportunity for people to join Rawleigh's sales network and to do well. Rawleigh will provide everything you will need to start you own venture including full training. The company's multi-level marketing plan has been designed to create a climate in which anybody, regardless of their financial circumstances, can succeed as long as they are prepared to work. Terry Rawleigh's marketing plan cuts out much of the paperwork. **He says multi-level marketing is "the last frontier for the average person to be able to get into business on his or her own".** This is because there are no large up front expenses.

RELIV

RELIV AUSTRALIA
Fred Cameron
Level 2, 80 Phillip Street
PARRAMATTA, NSW 2150
Telephone: (02) 687 1188
Fax: (02) 687 1202

RELIV USA
Robert L. Montgomery - CEO
Box 405, CHESTERFIELD
MO 630060405 USA
Telephone: (314) 537 9715
Fax: (314) 537 9753

MISSION STATEMENT

'Nourishing our world.'

COMPANY HISTORY

The product was created by Dr Ted Kalogris who developed Reliv's Classic Now. Responsible for 17 different patents during the past 40 years, Dr Kalogris turned his attention to the areas of nutrition and weight loss in 1978. Drawing on his years of experience, he has focused on key substances he believes are critical to permanent weight loss. He has evolved Ultrim Plus which he says is the best approach for healthy, permanent weight reduction. **Surveys show the number one New Year's resolution is to 'Lose Weight' and the second most popular resolution is to 'Make More Money'.** Reliv offers the opportunity for both. In the US, the company has grown from $1 million in its first full year to doing more than US$40 million in 1992. This is still a ground floor opportunity.

PRODUCTS

Reliv has a line of focused products featuring pure, high-quality ingredients. The NOW is a nutritional food supplement. Ultrim Plus has proved to be a successful weight loss program. Reliv's Now contains no additives, no yeast, fillers, preservatives or tablets. It contains 72 vitamins, minerals and herbs that have been designed to work in harmony with your body.

MARKETING PLAN

Most people become involved with Reliv by using the product and finding it works for them. In sharing the product with others they provide a valuable service and generate additional income. There are three ways of making money through Reliv:

1. **Retail profit.** Distributors can earn 25-45 per cent profit on products sold at suggested retail prices.

2. **Wholesale profit**. Affiliates can earn 5-20 per cent commission on personally-sponsored associates in their group.

3. **Generation of royalties.** Master affiliates receive a 2-5 per cent override on personally-sponsored master affiliates and their groups who have broken away.

Direct selling is a proven and well-respected method of moving products from the manufacturer to the end user who is the retail customer. The nutrition business is a billion dollar industry, and growing as the **baby boomers become more conscious of middle age.** There are no limits on what you can earn as a Reliv distributor. In March 1992, Success Magazine named **Reliv as the number one hot opportunity in network marketing.**

UNDERCOVER UNDERWEAR

UNDERCOVER UNDERWEAR
Kathy Hood
Box 1000, CASTLE HILL, NSW 2154
Telephone: (02) 634 3800
Fax: (02) 899 4874

MISSION STATEMENT

'To save others from suffering'. **The company increases awareness of breast cancer by distributing information on this curable disease at lingerie parties.** Through this it is hoped women will be prevented from dying unnecessarily.

COMPANY HISTORY

Kathy Hood started Undercover Underwear in Sydney, Australia in 1981. She now employs 1,600 agents and has an annual turnover of $16 million. Kathy who established the company on sound business principles, has tripled its size since 1990.

PRODUCTS

To cater for all tastes, sizes and occasions, Undercover lingerie ranges from sweet to sensual, and from naughty to nice. All product is made in Australia and is exclusive to Undercover. There is a new range three times a year.

MARKETING PLAN

All sales are conducted on a party plan system. Consultants get 20 per cent commission on sales. Managers get 24 per cent and unit managers receive a further bonus. Kathy encourages the parties to be held in a spirit of fun and entertainment. There is no limit to earning capacity. **You do not collect money or make deliveries.** It is easy to go into business with a starter kit made up of the top-selling garments for no cash outlay. The price of the kit is deducted from the first commission cheque if you can organise five parties in two weeks.

TRAINING

Regular training sessions and promotional material are provided. A manager in each state trains and administers the teams.

RECOGNITION, REWARDS, INCENTIVES

Undercover Underwear has prizes of overseas holidays.

WORLD BOOK

WORLD BOOK AUSTRALIA
Deborah Page
Level 1, 154 Pacific Highway
ST LEONARDS NSW 2065
Telephone: 61 2 439 3400
Fax: 61 2 439 4289

WORLD BOOK EDUCATIONAL
PRODUCTS USA
Frank Gagliardi
101 North West Point Boulevarde
ELK COVE VILLAGE ILLINOIS 60007
Telephone: 708 290 5300
Fax: 708 290 5301

MISSION STATEMENT

To provide the finest education materials to as many people as possible with the realisation that an educated child is a nation's greatest asset.

COMPANY HISTORY

World Book Australia was established in 1963. Mountain climber, Sir Edmund Hillary was actively involved as a director and held this position for 20 years. Although well-known overseas, World Book was a new name to most Australians. Today, more than 40,000 sets of World Book encyclopedia have been placed in Australian schools and libraries and more than 500,000 homes have World Book products.

World Book Australia operates through independent licensees in 27 designated territories throughout the country. Currently there are 18 licensees who have a combined strength of 2500 independent educational sales consultants.

World Book, Inc is one of the world's leading educational publishers. The company is based in Chicago and apart from the US, has operations in Australia, Britain, Canada and Ireland. There is also a network of worldwide distributors who sell in more than 50 other countries.

PRODUCTS

The 22-volume World Book encyclopedia is the company's major publication. It was first published in 1917 and has become the world's largest-selling encyclopedia. In 1922 it was published in a special international edition. Other major products are the two-volume World Book dictionary, 19-volume Childcraft, a reference set for pre-school to upper primary and Early World of Learning, a program for pre-school children. The company also markets an atlas, science encyclopedia and other supplementary publications which include the World Book Year Book which has annual sales of more than one million copies.

MARKETING PLAN

Licensees of World Book Australia have varying sponsorship programs. These are usually in the form of cash or merchandise items to the sponsor, with ongoing rewards as the new recruit achieves results.

The opportunity to sit with parents and discuss their children and their children's education and to provide the world's finest educational material at a very reasonable price makes World Book special.

TRAINING

A comprehensive training program is available to all independent educational sales consultants. There are continuing refresher programs for those who wish to participate. Local and international conferences also include opportunities for further training.

RECOGNITION, REWARDS, INCENTIVES

Licensees are paid commission based on results achieved. They establish levels of commission and bonuses for their independent educational sales consultants. Licensees also offer merchandise and travel rewards as additional incentives. World Book Australia sponsors four major sales contests and attendance at a local and an international conference.

'New World Bookers' have a chance to progress through a maximum of three levels from independent educational sales consultant to regional educational sales consultant. The basis of promotion is their ability to sell personally, recruit, train and motivate people to achieve. Each of World Book Australia's licensees began as educational sales consultants, although this is not a prerequisite.

DIRECT SELLING ASSOCIATIONS

MISSION STATEMENT:

To promote and protect the direct selling industry, its ideals and opportunities within each country.

DSA Australia
John Fulton
Suite 1, 13 Business Park Drive
NOTTING HILL, VICTORIA, 3168.
Phone: (03) 558 9352
Fax: (03) 558 9356

DSA New Zealand
Jeremy McLoughlin
Box 28245
REMEURA Auckland S
Phone: (9) 520 2044
Fax: (9) 523 3613

DSA USA
1776 K. Street N.W.
Suite 600 WASHINGTON DC 20006
Phone: (202) 293 5760
Fax: (202) 463 4569

DSA South Africa
c/- Johannesburg
Chamber of Commerce
Private Bag 34
Auckland park 2006
Phone: (11) 726 5300
Fax: (11) 726 8421

OTHER DIRECT SELLING COMPANIES

ADMARK SYSTEMS PTY LTD
Denis O'Donnell
1/22 Success Street
ACACIA RIDGE QLD 4110
Telephone: (07) 274 2198
Fax: (07) 277 1437
Perfume

ADVANCED LIFE FOODS
Phillip Crockford
24 Delvan Street
MANSFIELD
Telephone: (07) 849 5599
Fax: (07) 343 6931
Healthy foods, hair care and household products

BESSEMER PARTY PLAN
David McLean - Managing Director
141 Broadarrow Road
BEVERLEY HILLS NSW 2209
Telephone: (02) 534 6255
Fax: (02) 534 4322
Pots, pans, cookware

CHILDS PLAY LTD
Gary McManus - Managing Director
P.O. Box 209
TERREY HILLS NSW 2084
Telephone: (02) 450 2050
Fax: (02) 480 3225
Program of children's books, toys and games.

COBRA IMPORT EXP PROP LTD
Chris Niarchas, Sue Wright
76 Hargraves Place
WETHERILL PARK NSW 2164
Telephone: (02) 725 4100
Fax: (02) 725 4250
Stationery, houseware, books and toys, giftware.

DOMINANT (AUSTRALIA) PTY LTD
Christopher Short
12 Coglin Street
BROMPTON SA 5007
Telephone: (08) 346 8301
Fax: (08) 340 1626
Laundry, household and general cleaning products.

ELEMENTS AND ADD-ONS PTY LTD
Melinda Muth
685-689 Military Road
MOSMAN NSW 2088
Telephone: (02) 968 1149
Fax: (02) 968 1902
Ladies Fashions

ESSENTIAL ADDITIONS
Christian Jahnke
73 Upper Heidelberg Road
IVANHOE VIC 3079
Telephone: (03) 817 1161
Ladies handbags and fashion accessories

FILTER QUEEN AUST PTY LTD
Kevin McWilliams
27 Crescent Road
WARATAH NSW 2298
Telephone: (049) 601 155
Fax: (049) 601 868
Home sanitation systems

FURLONG WINE TASTINGS
John Furlong Senior
92 McEvoy Street
ALEXANDRIA NSW 2015
Telephone: (02) 699 4200
Fax: (02) 690 1603
Wines

LADY LOVE MANICURE COSMETICS PTY LTD
Hilton Wilson
66 Halidon Street
KINGSLEY WA 6062
Telephone: (09) 309 1010
Fax: (09) 309 4636
Fine products for manicure, nail art, lips and fragrance.

LEISURE FUN
Brian Quinn
Box 231 VERMONT VIC 3133
Telephone: (03) 874 8733
Fax: (03) 874 8309
Educational games, toys and jigsaws. Party plan. Established 15 years. 300 consultants.

LUX PTY LTD
Jim Ingamells
635 Waverley Road
GLEN WAVERLEY VIC 3150
Telephone: (03) 566 5200
Fax: (03) 561 4624
Household appliances including mainly vacuum cleaners

NIAGARA THERAPY MFG
Peter Crealey
4 Dan Street
SLACKS CREEK QLD 4127
Telephone: (07) 208 8788
Fax: (07) 208 5884
Massage equipment

NATURAL DECOR
Anne Edwards
23 Dividend Street
MANSFIELD QLD 4122
Telephone: (07) 849 2202
Fax: (07) 849 2205
Party plan linen and manchester, home decor and pottery. About 100 consultants.

NEOLIFE
Garry Walls, Gerry Krause
P.O. Box 419
BEENLEIGH QLD 4207
Telephone: (07) 807 3499
Fax: (07) 805 2728
Nutritional products, water and air filters.

NEW IMAGE INTERNATIONAL (AUST)
Kim Cambell, Sue Kenyon
110 Rocky Point Road
KOGARAH NSW 2317
Telephone: (02) 587 9800
Fax: (02) 587 9999
New Zealand based company. Nutrition and health products. Branches in Singapore, Taiwan, Malaysia and Indonesia.

OMEGATREND PTY LTD
CEO John Kenyon
216 Stirling Highway
CLAREMONT WA
Telephone: (09) 347 6200
Fax: (09) 347 6277
Perth based company. Household cleaning, skin-care and nutritional products.

O.T.T. FASHION CO PTY LTD
Julie Pillon
Suite 3, 202 Jersey Road
WOOLLAHRA NSW 2025
Telephone: (02) 363 1110
Fax: (02) 327 8424
O.T.T. Fashion, collection of stylish classical clothes. Party plan with multilevel remuneration.

POSTIE FASHIONS PTY LTD
Stephen Wilson
60-63 Lipps Street
COLLINGWOOD VIC 3067
Telephone: (03) 417 3900
Fax: (03) 416 2941
Selected women's fashions.

PRINCESS HOUSE AUST PTY LTD
Rob Lane
2 Hudson Avenue
CASTLE HILL NSW 2154
Telephone: (02) 634 4766
Fax: (02) 680 4398
Glassware and crystal.

SAN MICHELE FASHIONS PTY LTD
Sandra Plant
P.O. Box 741
DANDENONG VIC 3175
Telephone: (03) 720 6855
Fax: (03) 561 1009
Cosmetics, skincare products and fashion garments.

SILVER SWAN JEWELLERY
Bob Claxton - Managing Director
Locked Bag No. 1
TUART HILL WA 6060
Telephone: (09) 344 155
Fax: (09) 344 5311
Classic collection of genuine sterling silver, 9ct and 18ct gold jewellery.

SUNRIDER
Jeff Smith - General Manager
Dr Tei Su Chen - Founder
549 St Kilda Road
MELBOURNE VIC 3004
Telephone: (03) 526 4114
Fax: (03) 526 4115
Nutritional food supplements of herbal origin. 26,000 distributors in Australia, head office in Southern California, branches in 13 countries.

THE WICKED LADY
Wendy James - Director
Box 482
ST MARYS NSW 2760
Telephone: (02) 625 5817
Lingerie and naughty novelties.

TUPPERWARE AUSTRALIA PTY LTD
Fernando Monfort
465 Auburn Road
HAWTHORN VIC 3122
Telephone: (03) 822 0377
Fax: (03) 822 8928
Food containers and utility items.

UNIVERSAL ENERGY PRODUCTS
Helga Davis
12 Military Road
WATSONS BAY NSW 2030
Telephone: (02) 337 1849
Cream, shampoos, energy oils, energy mixtures, aphrodisiacs.

WIZKIDS BY GIVONI
Paul Givoni
212 Bay Road
SANDRINGHAM VIC 3191
Telephone: (03) 598 6955
Fax: (03) 598 0249
Children's clothing.

GLOSSARY

- Sponsor — To introduce someone to the business and to train and develop them.
- Network — A range of contacts.
- Network marketing — To develop a direct selling business through personal introductions.
- Recruit — A person newly enlisted into the company but not yet trained.
- Prospecting — Searching for new business or recruits.
- Commissions — A percentage of the value of product sold, paid to the agent.
- Multi-level — The system whereby the product reaches the end consumer via multi-tiered management structure.
- Party — A product demonstration, usually in the home or workplace. So called from the traditional Tupperware Party.
- Distributor — Agent/demonstrator, beauty consultant/ salesperson. A variety of terms to describe the direct selling independent retail commission agent i.e. independent (not employed) agent taking orders for a commission on behalf of the direct selling retailer.
- Distributorship — The independent business built by a distributor.
- Product — The goods or services on offer.
- Incentive — Encouragement by reward.
- Pyramid selling — A fraud. An illegal marketing plan built on the chain letter principle. People are invited to buy into a marketing scheme through large financial outlay. The purchase of a substantial amount of product on the inducement of being rewarded for introducing others into the scheme is also illegal.
  Contrast this with a legitimate marketing plan where the only rewards are sales made to the consumer, or a bonus from the sales of other people you have recruited and trained. No sale; no reward.
- Direct selling — The retailing of a product directly to the consumer on a person-to-person basis, primarily through independent retail sales agents, other than from a retail store.
  Not to be confused with Direct Marketing which is the term used to denote sales to the home/office by mail order, telephone, telemarketing etc., rather than through people.

ORGANISATIONS FOR NETWORKING

WOMEN AND MANAGEMENT INC
Sydney Division
Secretariat Box 647
ARTARMON NSW 2064
Telephone: (02) 412 3434
Fax: (02) 419 7561
Contact: **Maureen Downes**

AUSTRALIAN EXECUTIVE WOMEN'S NETWORK
PO Box 6090
Halifax St, ADELAIDE SA 5000
Telephone: (08) 232 1469
Fax: (02) 232 0488
Branches in all capital cities.
National Co-ordinator **Lucille D'Orr**

AUSTRALIAN FEDERATION OF BUSINESS AND PROFESSIONAL WOMEN
6th Floor, 141 Elizabeth St
SYDNEY NSW 2000
Branches all over Australia.
Telephone: (02) 267 5222
Or (060) 41 8861
Mary Callaway

SWAP
Contact **Graeme Nicholls**
PO Box 668 Broadway 2007
Telephone: (02) 368 1678
Fax: (02) 368 1678
Meets once a week in all capital cities.

BRISBANE CIRCLE
Networking Publication for Women in Brisbane.
Editor **Di Watson**
PO Box 127
TOOWONG 4066 Qld
Telephone: (07) 371 7537
Fax: (07) 378 3077

THE EXECUTIVE WOMAN'S REPORT
Editor **Margaret Christie**
Windsor Business Centre
2/3 Wellington Street
WINDSOR VIC 3181
Telephone: (03) 529 5655
Fax: (03) 529 6994

WOMEN AND MANAGEMENT
Western Australia
PO Box 195
WEMBLEY WA 6014
Telephone: (09) 387 7788
Fax: (09) 387 6171

INTERNATIONAL TRAINING IN COMMUNICATION (ITC)
CHATSWOOD NSW
Telephone: (02) 985 0279
Branches throughout Australia.

TOASTMASTERS
(02) 790 2986
List of 150 clubs available.
Teaches skills in public speaking

ZONTA INTERNATIONAL
5 Wentworth Avenue
DARLINGHURST NSW 2010
Telephone: (02) 264 2451
Branches throughout Australia.

NATIONAL SPEAKERS ASSOCIATION OF AUSTRALIA
NSW Chapter
Telephone: (02) 959 5803
Contact **Brendon Walsh**

BUSINESS PLUS
MONEY AND YOU CREATING WEALTH WORKSHOPS
PO Box 42
GLEBE NSW 2037
Telephone: (02) 552 1188
Fax: (02) 552 4954
Contact: **James Caldwell** – Director

FOREWORD TO RECOMMENDED READING

I have spent three months writing and researching this book. Writing is a very lonely process. It takes total focus and solitary involvement to sit in isolation and actually write a book. I have had a wonderful three months. I have been surrounded by a circle of warm, intimate friends. Friends who have supported, inspired and revealed great insights to me. They have stimulated and shared common thoughts, feelings and revelations. These friends are the authors of the books I recommend. I feel enriched by having read their work. I hope my book **reflects** the depth of their input. I encourage you to read as many as you can. They will enrich your life as they have enriched mine.

RECOMMENDED READING

All I Really Needed To Know I
Learned In Kindergarten
Robert Fulghum
Grafton Books, 1990

Assertive Woman, The
Stanlee Phelps, Nancy Austin MBA
Impact Publishers, California, 1987

Being Happy, A Handbook To
Greater Confidence And Security
Andrew Mathews
Media Masters, 1990

Being The Best You Can In MLM
John Kalench
MIM Publications, 1990

Beauty Myth, The
Naomi Wolf
Vintage, London, 1990

Body And Soul
Anita Roddick
Ebury Press, London, 1991

Creative Visualisation
Gawain Skakti
Bantam Books, NY, 1978

Dance Of Intimacy, The
Harriet Goldhor Lerner Phd
Harper and Row, 1989

Feel The Fear And Do It Anyway
Susan Jeffers
Arrow Books, London, 1987

Get What You Want
Patricia Fripp
HDL Communications, USA, 1988

If You Want To Be Rich and Happy
Don't Go To School
Robert T. Kiyosaki
The Accelerated Learning Publishing
Company, 1992

Making Friends, A Guide To Getting
Along With People
Andrew Mathews
Media Masters, 1990

Mary Kay
Mary Kay
Harper and Row, NY, 1987

Network Marketing, Another Form Of
Direct Sales
**Elizabeth Kearney Phd, Michale
Bandley Phd**
Business Education Institute,
Melbourne 1988

Never Underestimate The Selling
Power Of A Woman
Dottie Walters
Wilshire Book Company, 1986

New Woman's Survival Guide, The
Linda Hughes Allen
Acropolis Books, USA

Nothing Ventured, Nothing Gained
Fabian Dattner
Penguin Books, 1992

One Minute Manager, The
**Kenneth Blanchard Phd and Spencer
Johnson Phd**

Party Your Way To Prosperity, A
Complete Guide To Party Plan
Selling
Helen Bruveris
Millennium Books, Australia, 1991

Path Finders
Gail Sheehy
Bantam Books, 1981

People Management
Mary Kay
Warner Books, 1984

Raising Positive Kids In A Negative
World
Zig Ziglar
Thomas Nelson, USA, 1985

Really Relating
David Jansen, Margaret Newman
Random House, Australia, 1989

Revolution From Within
Gloria Steinem
Bloomsbury Publishing, 1992

Speak And Grow Rich
Dottie and Lily Walters
Prentice Hall, USA, 1989

Successful Woman, The
Dr Joyce Brothers
Ballentine Books, NY, 1988

Super Confidence, The Woman's
Guide To Getting What You Want Out
Of Life
Gael Lindenfield
Thorsons Publishing, Great Britain,
1989

Tall Poppies Too
Susan Mitchell
Penguin Books, Australia, 1991

The Seven Habits Of Highly Effective
People
Steven Covey
Simon and Schuster, USA, 1991

Think And Grow Rich
Napoleon Hill
Melvin Powers, California, 1937

You Can Heal Your Life
Louise L. Hay
Specialist Publications, 1984

What Smart Women Know, Wisdom
For The Thinking Woman
Steven Carter, Julia Sokol
Dell Publishing, NY, 1990

ABOUT THE AUTHOR

Cyndi Kaplan is a successful author, speaker, designer and entrepreneur. She is managing director of Godiva Publishing Pty Ltd which was established in 1989. She has an arts degree with a major in Psychology.

From 1977 to 1989 Cyndi set up a business called Nikkikraft, designing, manufacturing and marketing creative activity toys. Cyndi sold her toys to all leading supermarkets in Australia as well as exported her designs to Europe, USA, Canada and New Zealand. The Nikkikraft range is now in its 10th year in Australia and is being distributed under licence by Kidz Korner Pty Ltd, based in Sydney.

In 1989 Cyndi wrote and published her first book, **There's a Lipstick in my Briefcase**, a guide for the New Woman Entrepreneur. The book was based on her own personal experience in the international business arena where Cyndi developed her varied expertise in sales, marketing and product development.

The book has been very well received in Australia, New Zealand and South Africa. It is now in its fourth reprint. The book is used as a reference book in small business studies at all TAFEs and Business colleges. It is also used by the Small Business Development Corporations in all states.

During 1990-91 Cyndi travelled extensively throughout Australia lecturing and motivating women in all areas of business. She was amazed at the number of talented women she met in the Direct Selling business. This stimulated her desire to write a book to promote the Direct Selling industry.

Cyndi's mission is to inspire, encourage and motivate women to develop their potential and achieve financial independence.

Cyndi's public speaking talents are in great demand throughout Australia. Cyndi is available for conferences, seminars and conventions and may be booked by contacting her agent Harry M. Miller Speaker's Bureau (02) 357 3077 or fax (02) 356 2880.

ENDORSEMENTS

"**The Beauty of Business** is one of the brightest and most refreshing manuscripts I've ever read – pacey, easy to read and extremely motivational."

Bill Duncan
CORPORATE AFFAIRS MANAGER
AMWAY OF AUSTRALIA PTY LTD.

"**The Beauty of Business** is full of information on starting a business in the direct selling industry especially for the lay person who is just beginning. The book has a tremendous amount of training material. I could hardly put it down."

Sherien Foley
EXECUTIVE DIRECTOR
PRO-MA SYSTEMS INCORPORATING GRACE COSMETICS

"Fantastic book! Compulsory reading for anyone looking seriously at M.L.M. as well as for those already in the industry."

Tom and Elfie Reiner
HERBALIFE DISTRIBUTORS

"A very practical guide for the modern Australian woman who has made the decision to secure her financial future through the power of multilevel marketing."

Laraine Richardson
HERBALIFE INTERNATIONAL
PRESIDENT'S TEAM MEMBER

"**The Beauty of Business** is an excellent handbook containing an objective analysis of opportunities in the direct selling industry."

Marcia Griffin
GENERAL MANAGER
POLA SKINCARE, COSMETICS

"**The Beauty of Business** is a realistic handbook for anyone contemplating a career in direct sales and a good reminder of the basic principles for those already involved."

Gillian Chan
MARY KAY COSMETICS
SALES DIRECTOR